THE
MORTGAGE
MARKETING
MANIFESTO

THE MORTGAGE MARKETING MANIFESTO

*Unlocking the Holy Grail of
Mortgage Lead Generation*

ANDREW PAWLAK

Dedication

To my wife and soulmate, Ashley. For the last 11 years, you've been my rock and inspiration.

To my dad, who taught me to work hard and inspired me to become an entrepreneur.

To my partner, Robert Shuey, who helped me build leadPops.

And to Riley, my beloved "Lead Pup"—Best Dog Ever.

Contents

Part 2: Your Next 275 Days & Beyond

Foreword

by Ryan Stewman,
CEO at Hardcore Closer

The days of taking rate sheets and doughnuts to the local Realtor® office in order to get loans are gone. Unless you're talking gluten-free doughnuts... Nah, who am I kidding? Realtors® don't want those either.

In the modern marketplace, you've got to be different; not just better at the same old spiel that others have been using for decades.

For the last thirteen years of my life, I've been heavily involved with the mortgage industry. In the last six years alone, I've worked with nearly 1,000 MLOs who close more than $2M each month in volume.

Not a single one of them chases real estate agents. They don't even chase prospects.

They advertise and let the leads chase them.

In my career as an internet marketer, I've created over 2,000 sales funnels. I've tested, split-tested, and re-tested more variations of copy and placement to find the optimal prospect-centered solution as many times, or more, than Edison undertook in his 10,000 attempts to create the light bulb.

Six months ago, I was introduced to Andrew Pawlak and <u>leadPops</u>, and it was as if the light bulb had been reinvented!

It has been my experience that most MLOs fail at advertising and lead generation because they don't understand it.

You don't sell a mortgage or a rate. No one wants either of those. What you sell is the security of living in a home the client desires at a payment they can comfortably afford.

No one cares about the LO or the interest rate. They care about your ability to keep them from being homeless.

The average LO's age is fifty-three. Most don't have a prolific background in technology, either.

As a matter of fact, the majority of LOs are so busy closing loans that they don't have the time to figure out fancy programs and software.

Yet, without the right tools and technology, LOs will have an incredibly hard time consistently generating qualified leads and making their marketing work the way it should.

The days of cold calling are gone—and let's be honest, no one will miss them!

Think about it: we have the National Do Not Call Registry, the CAN-SPAM Act and various other regulations, all of which deter strangers from bugging consumers.

Yet, many LOs still believe in cold calls and the old doughnut/rate sheet drop-in...

I'm not saying those don't ever work; I'm saying they suck and are a HUGE waste of time.

The future is now, and generating inbound leads from online sources has replaced the cold call.

It's a different way to conduct business, and an exciting way. Wouldn't you rather only talk to people who want to talk to you?

It's hard to get hung up on when the people you're reaching out to are asking to speak with you!

That is the goal—for starters—isn't it? Only talking to people that want to speak with you and are expecting your call?

And that's where leadPops comes in. It makes creating funnels—digital mechanisms for capturing qualified leads—so easy *any LO* can build 30+ funnels in less than 60 seconds and start generating leads the same day.

Still, many of you reading this are likely using websites like Trulia, Zillow, LendingTree, and Lower My Bills as lead resources... Instead of generating your own leads.

There's a reason Zillow is the king of real estate online. They understand lead generation, and control millions of leads monthly.

That's why tons of Realtors® turn to Zillow as a lead source... Internet marketing is hard and complicated. It's far easier when agents leave all that to someone else.

And make no mistake about it, most of you probably think the way it works is Realtors® are supposed to give loan officers referrals... Not the other way around.

It doesn't have to, and shouldn't be that way.

Today, there is something new—and the strategies taught by Andrew in this book will show you the exact methods and technology the big boys use to generate millions of mortgage and real estate leads each month...

And the best part is: it's stuff you could be doing yourself, and it's now available to you for way less than buying one zip code or an "exclusive" lead.

When you have the ability to generate leads at will, Realtors® will come to you as the originator who feeds *them* leads. After all, agents' favorite radio station is WIIFM: what's in it for me!

If you provide a solid agent with buyer/seller leads, you'll find that loyalty issues are a thing of the past.

They will send you every good deal they get... And will continue to do so as long as the referrals are a 2-way street, vs. the agent always feeding the loan officer business.

This means no more MSAs (or whatever they call them legally these days) and no more co-marketing with agents. Which is just vernacular for, "Pay some of my bills for me."

You, the LO, will be in control of which agent gets what lead, and who you want to do business with.

Once you generate your own leads and close your own sales, you step into a space of power very few experience.

The Mortgage Marketing Manifesto is the blueprint you need in order to become a lead-generating, loan-closing machine, without having to chase agents or prospects.

Instead, they will be chasing YOU.

In the following pages, you will learn about strategies, tools, and tactics that have led to millions in commissions for a lot of well-to-do loan officers.

You'll be able to get a behind-the-scenes look at how technology works, and how you can easily put it to work for you.

The key, though, is to actually implement the ideas you'll learn about as you read this book—it's a career changer!

No plan comes together without action.

My good pal, Andrew, has put his expertise to work in writing this book and creating leadPops.

He's one of the best in the industry, and through this information, you will become empowered in your marketplace.

You will be able to take your business to a level you've never before experienced, and one which you've only dreamed of since the day you took your first loan app.

So enjoy the book. Implement the plan. Reap the benefits.

—Ryan Stewman

Ryan Stewman is a nationally renowned sales and marketing trainer for the mortgage and real estate industries, among others.

As the CEO of Hardcore Closer and Break Free Academy, Ryan has been featured on Inc.com, Entrepreneur.com, and recognized by the Huffington Post as one of the "Top 6 Facebook Marketers To Follow" in 2016.

Learn more about Ryan at www.HardcoreCloser.com

Introduction

I wrote this book to help loan officers and mortgage brokers who are hustling to generate business <u>shatter</u> the barriers that are preventing them from closing more loans.

Whether it's because:

- ► You're not getting the ROI you should be from your marketing efforts;
- ► You've got a revolving door of Realtors®;
- ► You're struggling with consistency; or,
- ► You want to take your business to the next level and have hit a ceiling...

If any (or all) of these describe your situation, this book will help.

The fact is that the information I share in this *Manifesto* can change your life.

You might be thinking, "That sounds pretty deep for a book on mortgage marketing."

... Well, it is.

Ask yourself this: how would things be different if I started consistently closing 2, 3, 5, 8, 10, 12+ *additional* loans per month?

I dare say that'd be a life-changing phenomenon; wouldn't you agree?

Execute on the ideas I share in this *Manifesto* and you will drastically improve the ROI on just about <u>everything</u> you do going forward as a mortgage professional for the rest of your career.

Now you might be thinking, "This sounds like BS."

... Well, it isn't.

You're going to see that for yourself.

Of course, you have every right to be skeptical.

There's a lot of crap out there in the mortgage world—companies and people that make big promises, but always under deliver.

I know because I've been working in the trenches with mortgage and real estate professionals for over 12 years now.

Let's back up.

My name is Andrew Pawlak. I'm the Co-Founder & CEO @ leadPops.com.

I started out in the industry when I was 19, cold-calling Realtors® and selling digital marketing packages for one of the fastest growing real estate marketing companies in San Diego, back in 2004.

I came to the realization very early in my career that websites and marketing are pointless if they're not converting quality leads and helping clients make sales.

Since then, I've co-founded 2 top-tier mortgage marketing technology companies.

Over the years, the technology and strategies I've developed have helped my clients generate millions of leads and *close* well over 100,000 transactions.

Having worked with loan officers, mortgage brokers, mortgage bankers, and Realtors® for the last decade plus—I've pretty much seen it all.

I know what works and what doesn't.

My goal is to teach you what I know about mortgage marketing and lead generation, and to do it in a way that's easy to follow and thorough, yet concise.

I'm going to train you to be a smarter, more effective marketer *and* business person.

By the time you get to the end of this book, if you read everything and pay close attention, I can guarantee you absolutely will be better at what you do.

You'll have an unfair advantage over all the other LOs and mortgage brokers you're competing with in your market for business.

But first, I need to "rewire" the way you think about marketing and business development.

You can't look at digital marketing as being separate from your offline marketing and referral generation efforts.

Events, business cards, direct mail, Realtor® relationships, social media, radio ads, websites, signage, marketing to past clients, landing pages, emails, etc.—

It's all interconnected.

It's all one.

And all of it needs to be *optimized* and *integrated* to get the desired results.

I'm going to show you how to do exactly that.

I'll teach you to take a "results-driven" approach to your marketing and business development efforts, rather than just wasting time and money throwing stuff out there and hoping something sticks.

If you're struggling to hit your goals and just doing 1-4 loans per month, the knowledge you will gain in the pages of this book can help you double, triple, and even quadruple your results. Perhaps even beyond that!

If you're doing 5-10 loans per month currently, this book can help you double that in 90 days or less.

But only if you execute.

Fact is: if you implement even a handful of the ideas I share in this *Manifesto*, you will see a drastic improvement in your lead quantity, quality, and most importantly, sales.

By the way, if you're doing 11-20 loans per month or more, and you have the desire and capacity to increase that number—fantastic. I can help you double that, too.

Let's put you in a position where you're only taking on the loans and types of clients and business partners you want to work with.

Again, this might sound like BS to you—that's OK.

I understand.

I'd think so too, if I was you.

But then, I would also read this entire book before drawing my conclusion.

So I challenge you to read this *Manifesto* in its entirety.

See if you don't come out the other end with more knowledge and actionable ideas on how to grow your mortgage business than ever before.

I'm not going to try to convince you to buy anything from me, either.

That's not why I wrote this book.

Sure, I make references to some of the solutions that my company builds, but make no mistake—I don't talk about them because we build them... we build them because they're integral to the success of any mortgage professional that's looking to take their business to the next level.

This book contains 35 chapters of mortgage marketing strategies and insights to help you take your business further.

I'm going to share a ton of stuff you've never seen or heard anywhere else.

In the process, I'd also like to expose the "big dog" players in the mortgage industry.

You know who I'm talking about...

Companies like LendingTree, LowerMyBills, Zillow, Trulia, and many more of the mortgage industry's mega lead mongers.

They know of a "top secret" method to get the most out of all of their marketing dollars...

They've spent the last decade or more, and hundreds of millions of dollars on marketing, in research and development, and testing, to figure out how to convert qualified mortgage leads consistently—at the highest rate possible.

But they're not going to tell you about it.

The last thing they want is for loan officers and mortgage brokers to figure out the methods they use to generate their leads.

You see, they want to keep people relying on them for business.

That way they can continue selling their old, stinky fish leads—day after day, week after week, month after month, year after year—as long as loan officers and brokers keep showing up to their docks...

Well, how about this crazy idea, instead?

Let's teach YOU how to fish.

After all, you're already in the boat, and you've even got a rod with a line dangling in the water...

The problem is you've got no bait and you've got no hook.

The fish are swimming all around, but unless they jump into your boat, your chances of catching anything are slim to none.

Here's what I'm saying:

I'm very good at "fishing"... You might even call me a "master angler".

In 2013, I was contracted by Zillow to help increase the amount of leads their clients were generating from Zillow's Mortgage Marketplace. Within just a few weeks, I was able to boost conversion rates across the board, even doubling them for many of their mortgage clients.

In 2014, I became THE preferred mortgage landing page and conversion optimization expert for Bankrate, ensuring their mortgage advertisers get the most out of every dollar they spend.

Now, helping billion dollar companies is cool and all, but I personally get the most satisfaction out of working with 1-2 person operations, and smaller teams and brokerages.

It's a lot more fulfilling (and fun) to help out the underdogs in a world where a handful of ginormous companies are hogging so much of the spotlight.

And that's why I've created this *Manifesto*... for you.

I've broken it up into 2 parts.

Part 1 will serve as a marketing plan and guide covering priorities for your first 90 days.

Part 2 offers additional, high-value marketing ideas and insights that will keep you busy closing additional loans for the rest of the year and well beyond.

Chapters 1 & 2 are the FOUNDATION of all your marketing efforts...

Without the right foundation, none of your marketing will produce the results it should.

Throughout this *Manifesto* you will find references to "Bonus".

These are additional resource guides that will expand to provide you with even more insight on the given topic.

Although these guides are usually only available to my clients, I've unlocked several of them for you at no cost in this *Manifesto*.

So, without further ado, let's get into the content that brought you here in the first place.

I recommend you turn off your phone. Close your email, Facebook, LinkedIn, etc.

Eliminate distractions and focus.

It's time to start making the kind of money you deserve while doing what you love.

PART 1

Your First 90 Days

CHAPTER 1

Launch a Mortgage Marketing Website That's Optimized to Convert Leads

I'm not talking about your grandmother's "digital brochure" mortgage website with a bunch of stuff to read, some pictures, and a loan application.

Don't get me wrong—I love Grandma... she's great, but she shouldn't be building your mortgage website.

Just like tech companies with <u>zero</u> understanding of marketing and lead generation shouldn't be building your mortgage website either.

Not if you're trying to generate business, that is.

In fact, using a digital brochure website (or not having a website) is a primary reason why so many mortgage professionals struggle with their marketing—both online and offline.

In order for your mortgage website to produce business, it needs to be powered by "conversion rate optimization", also known as CRO.

Conversion rate optimization is a method for increasing the percentage of potential clients that convert into customers, or more specifically, take a desired action on a website or landing page, or in response to an email, direct mail piece, social media post, radio ad, or any type of advertisement or offer.

It's important for you to understand that not all websites are created equal.

Just because a website looks nice doesn't mean it's capable of generating business.

If it's not built to convert traffic into leads, then it's costing you clients.

In a world where you can make anywhere from $1K to $5K+ per loan, just a handful of lost opportunities is a big deal.

Also, if you're not generating enough leads for yourself, how are you going to share leads with your Realtor® partners?

That's the Holy Grail when it comes to building loyal Realtor® relationships—you bringing *them* business vs. always chasing them around for referrals.

That's where CRO comes in.

You can't do business with clicks.

Potential clients, including referrals, are going to look you up online, usually *before* they call you.

They will Google your name and your company.

These days, people want to do some research before speaking with a salesperson, especially on a high-ticket item as critical as a mortgage/real estate transaction.

Just take a look at some of these statistics...

> *"97% of consumers go online to research products and services before purchasing locally."*
>
> **BIA/Kelsey**
> **Market Research Study**

"90%+ of homebuyers search online during their home buying process."

National Association of Realtors®
The Digital House Hunt Report

"Real estate related searches on Google have grown 253% over the past 4 years."

National Association of Realtors®
The Digital House Hunt Report

By the way, those 2 stats above from the National Association of Realtors® shed light on why real estate agents typically beat mortgage pros to hot homebuyer leads... But don't worry—I'm going show you how to flip that on its head later in this *Manifesto*.

"90% of consumers read online reviews before visiting a business."

Search Engine Land
BrightLocal Survey

"88% of consumers trust online reviews as much as personal recommendations."

Search Engine Land
BrightLocal Survey

As you can see, your potential clients are online.

You need to control what comes up in the search engines when potential clients are searching for you.

And what comes up needs to be optimized to convert clicks into qualified leads, not just a bunch of stuff to read about mortgages.

Without conversion rate optimization, you're losing tens of thousands of dollars in business each year.

And if you're doing a good amount of marketing—*make that per month.*

CRO should not be confused with SEO (search engine optimization), which can be helpful for *getting* traffic, but will also do nothing for you without conversion rate optimization.

Getting traffic without converting leads is like running the A/C with all your windows down, but a lot more costly.

Keep in mind, potential clients you miss out on aren't going to call to report to you that your lead generation strategy isn't working.

They just click around, then off your website or page and *disappear forever.* They don't abandon their search, either... They end up somewhere else.

You must start with a foundation that's built to capture and convert qualified leads, and all of your marketing will have a much better chance of showing you the positive ROI (return on investment) that you're looking for.

Watch this video I made for you at:

www.leadPops.com/big-dogs

It's going to show you exactly how some of the biggest companies in the mortgage industry are capturing qualified leads from their marketing efforts—***using websites with built-in landing pages that are optimized for conversion.***

Once you see how they're doing it, it becomes much easier to understand how you can use these exact same tactics and strategies to generate your own exclusive mortgage leads.

Without landing pages built into your website (like the ones I show you the big companies using in the video above, and those covered in detail in Chapter 2), all you have is a bunch of stuff to read and a loan application...

That's not going to cut it when you're competing with billion dollar companies who've spent hundreds of millions of dollars figuring out how to get as many leads as possible out of their marketing efforts.

A 1003 application only gets filled out when you direct people you're *already* working with to do so.

And "contact me" forms?

Those are not lead generators.

Contact forms are about as effective as "sign my guestbook" registration pages you used to see on websites back in the days of dial up modems.

Also, know this:

> **Just because you're not trying to actively drive people to your website or page doesn't mean they're not finding it on their own as a result of your marketing efforts, word-of-mouth, social media, emails, business cards, etc.**

The reason you're not getting anything out of it is because you don't have any engagement tools or CRO!

Google Analytics (covered later in this chapter) can help you determine how much traffic you're getting, which is crucial for measuring the effectiveness of your marketing.

And not to worry, I have some good news for you: when it comes to launching a powerful marketing website, it's a relatively easy fix since there's no need to reinvent the wheel.

You can simply replicate the strategies that the most successful companies in the mortgage industry are using to generate *your own* exclusive leads.

You also don't need a million dollar a day marketing budget…

But, if you want to compete with the big boys and WIN, you need to have the same equipment—otherwise you'll be sitting on the sidelines and you'll continue to miss out on clients you should be closing.

Bonus: I've built a demo mortgage website to serve as an example of the ideal mortgage marketing website setup:

www.MortgagePops.com

If you're going to build a new mortgage website or redesign your current site, that demo serves as a great blueprint to follow.

Important Mortgage Marketing Website Features

Here's a list of important features I recommend you consider incorporating into your mortgage marketing website:

Built-In Lead Generation Landing Pages for All Target Loan Types & Products

A mortgage website that has been optimized for marketing and lead conversion should include individual mortgage content pages with built-in lead capture landing pages for:

- ► 15 Year Fixed
- ► 203K Loans
- ► 30 Year Fixed
- ► ARMs

- ► Custom Rate Quotes
- ► FHA Loans
- ► HARP Loans
- ► Home Purchases
- ► Home Refinances
- ► Jumbo Loans
- ► New Construction Loans
- ► Reverse Mortgages
- ► USDA Loans
- ► VA Loans

Of course, only include the types of loans you want to focus on.

If there's anything missing from the list above that you want to go after, include a content page + a lead capture landing page for it, too.

Everything you need to know about mortgage landing pages is covered in Chapter 2.

Your Website Must Be 100% Mobile Responsive

40-50%+ of your traffic is mobile—don't miss out on half the market by having a website that doesn't dynamically respond and adapt to any size smartphone or tablet.

If you have a website, use this free Google tool to check if your website passes the mobile test:

www.leadPops.com/mobile-website-test

Feature a Customized "About" Section

Believe it or not, the "about" section of mortgage websites is one of the most popular when it comes to where consumers click. Don't leave yours with a canned paragraph provided by your template website company.

Not only is that lame, but those canned company spiels are typically used on dozens, if not hundreds of other websites, which can also hurt your search engine placement (duplicate content penalties).

The "about" section gives you a chance to separate yourself from all the mortgage call centers and other competitors who don't take the time to personalize this important client-getting tool.

Use the opportunity to introduce yourself—your experience, education, accomplishments, and even examples of how you've helped clients.

Tell a story that will attract the types of clientele and partners you want to work with.

Don't be afraid to make your "about" section personal by sharing details about what you like to do in your free time, family, sports, hobbies, etc.—that's what this section is all about (without going overboard, of course).

A picture of you and your golden retriever wearing matching Christmas sweaters? That might be a little much. Skip that.

You running a half marathon to raise money to help fight childhood obesity? That's pretty awesome. Include it.

Video can be another powerful way to further differentiate yourself and make a personal connection.

It doesn't need to be a fancy or expensive production—a simple web cam, a clean office as your background, and a smile is all you need.

If you do a video, be yourself and try not to sound scripted. This may sound easier said than done, but with a little practice, you'll get comfortable with it in no time.

60-90 seconds in length should be fine if you decide to shoot an "about" video.

As with ALL areas of your mortgage website, make sure the "about" section clearly links to a lead generation landing page offering a custom rate quote so that you can transition visitors from anonymous website viewers to conversations, and then clients.

Client & Partner "Reviews" Section

The stats I shared near the beginning of this *Manifesto*—90% of consumers read online reviews before visiting a business, and 88% of them trust online reviews as much as personal recommendations—both explain the importance of building a positive online reputation.

Your website provides you with an ideal platform to showcase success stories and testimonials from clients and partners you've helped.

It's especially powerful if the reviews also live on 3rd party websites like Yelp, Google+, Facebook, TrustPilot, etc.

Insider Tip: Zillow might seem like a great place to put a lot of reputation-building effort into, but I don't recommend putting all your eggs in their basket.

Keep in mind—Zillow pretty much competes with you and uses your content to grow their traffic and search engine rankings so they can capture more of your leads.

The last thing you want is for potential clients that are looking for you to find Zillow and get ensnared by one of their many mousetraps—you might end up buying a lead you should have converted yourself, or even worse, Zillow sells that lead to one of your competitors without you ever even knowing about it.

This is one of their tactics, by the way, so don't feed the monster.

There are all kinds of tricky ways companies like Zillow get unsuspecting mortgage pros and Realtors® to give up their traffic and leads to them for free.

That includes "free" widgets like badges and calculators they give mortgage pros and Realtors® to put on their websites...

Not only do those take users off of your website and drive them back to Zillow, but on top of that, they layer hidden search engine optimization tactics, like added links and keywords, into those widgets to further help them overpower you in Google for local mortgage related searches.

Lastly, there's a powerful tool for review collection and reputation management called SocialSurvey. They specialize in the mortgage space, and do an incredible job of engaging your clients—compelling your raving fans to share the story of their experience with you, online, for the world to see.

Their system also helps you resolve complaints, giving you an opportunity to fix issues and make them right by your customers.

There's no doubt, referrals are your best opportunity to get more clients, and SocialSurvey can help you get more of them.

I encourage you to check it out, and share it with your peers and/or management team. It's an Enterprise solution though, so your company will have to sign up at a corporate level. Once you see it in action, I think you'll understand why I've become such a fan.

Check out SocialSurvey for yourself, go to:

www.SocialSurvey.com (no affiliation to leadPops)

List Building Technology & Automated Email Follow-Up System

Building your email subscriber list is critical to growing your business.

Emails are the fastest, least expensive, and often most effective way to communicate with past clients, leads, and partners—allowing you to reach your entire database with a valuable message, promotion, new product, rate update, "just listed" property, open house, or anything you want to send out with just a click.

To automate your list building and future client interaction, make sure your marketing website integrates an email newsletter that also ties in your drips, autoresponders, and automation tools.

You can do this simply by adding an e-newsletter signup form to your homepage and other subpages of your website.

Just make sure you use a strong call-to-action to encourage people to signup, otherwise a request for an email address won't get much of a response.

You can also offer "lead magnets"—ethical bribes offering valuable content in exchange for desired information (like an email address)—in the form of free reports, eBooks, white papers, webinar signups, and more. All of these can be used to grow your subscriber list.

Lead magnets, coupled with list building tools like opt-in boxes, pop-ups, email-grabber bars, page takeovers, sliders, and exit intent triggers, can be an excellent way to build your list.

These simple list building tools can be added to any website and custom tailored to fit your requirements, meaning—they only show when you want them to, on the pages you want, and to the people you want to see them.

I provide a catalog of some of my favorite marketing technologies (including list building tools) in Chapter 34 of this *Manifesto*, so be sure to check those out.

Key Statistic:
"Email marketing has an R.O.I. of 4,300%."
Direct Marketing Association

"Trusted Pros" Referral Partner Showcase

Think of this as your local online concierge, or private yellow page directory that features only your best referral partners.

It's an excellent way to better service clients. By creating a "one-stop shop", you'll keep people on your website for longer periods of time, while offering a great value (free marketing and exposure) to your referral partners.

This becomes even more valuable to your referral partners when you explain what kind of marketing you're doing—the size of your database, email marketing, social media campaigns, SEO, PPC, radio ads, events, open houses, seminars, webinars, direct mail, etc.—any and all marketing efforts become additional talking points for you to ratchet up the perceived value of your offer to promote your partners as "Trusted Pros" on your website.

This kind of showcase packs additional, powerful benefits into your Unique Selling Proposition when recruiting new referral partners, like: Realtors®, builders, CPAs, attorneys, insurance agents, title reps, home stagers, home decorators, home inspectors, financial planners, landscapers, listing photographers, attorneys, appraisers, escrow agents, architects, pest control companies, solar companies, and all other professionals you work with, or simply know and have a relationship with.

This strategy will help you will establish loyalty and further separate you from other mortgage pros that are inevitably going to be speaking with, and trying to win over, <u>your</u> referral partners.

> **For maximum value, segment your referral partners into different territories broken up by geographic area and/ or niche.**

That way you can load up more referral partners while keeping your offering exclusive.

Make each partner the only "go-to person" in the _____ industry servicing a specific "territory" and/or niche and you'll be able to load up a couple dozen "Trusted Partners" in no time. The more the better!

Besides being a cool thing to do for your clients and referral partners, there's even more hidden value here...

Set this up right and leads that come through your website to your "Trusted Pros" get routed to both YOU and your select referral partners. Double whammy.

This also gives you an opportunity to get *your* website listed on *theirs* as a trusted local mortgage professional.

That means more free exposure for you.

Which is also why it's important to be selective with who you team up with as a 'Trusted Pro"—you don't want to load up a bunch of people that don't do any marketing and can't bring much value to the table or return the favor.

In addition, more links pointing to your website from relevant local websites can help your search engine rankings.

Important Note: Loading up referral partners should be as easy as emailing the website or LinkedIn profile of your new "Trusted Pro" to your website company, assistant or virtual assistant, or marketing manager.

The last thing you should be doing is spending a bunch of time playing website maintenance guy/gal.

Your job is building relationships and closing loans, not tinkering with websites, so don't get bogged down by the minutia.

Proper On-Page Search Engine Optimization (SEO)

Your website homepage and inner pages need to have the correct title tags, keywords, and descriptions.

These should include your geographic location—city/state—and a combination of mortgage-specific keywords, including but not limited to—mortgage, home loans, refinance, mortgage rates, VA loans, FHA loans, jumbo loans, etc.

Each page of your website with unique content should have unique title tags, keywords, and descriptions that reflect the content on that page + your location (city/town).

Your chances of coming up in the top 10 organically nationwide or for the entire state + a keyword, like mortgage or refinance, are pretty slim at this point... unless you have many thousands of dollars per month and a year or two to dedicate to the challenge (still, with no guarantees).

However, by focusing on your local city/specific location, you can increase your chances of placing well, especially for long-tail key phrases (longer, more specific keywords that potential clients are likely to use when they're closer to the point of purchase).

More on Mortgage SEO in Chapter 20

Secure Loan Application Center

A loan application isn't a lead generator, but it can be a great service tool (and time saver).

Also, considering how much of your business will come from millennials over the coming years, having a user-friendly, secure online loan application option for clients is a must.

A company that is doing some really cool things with their 1003 application technology is called www.Roostify.com—check them out (no affiliation to leadPops).

MLS Home Search Lead Generation Landing Page

Use an MLS search lead generation landing page to generate homebuyer leads for both you and your Realtor® partners.

Real estate searches get 5-100X more action online than anything mortgage related.

Check out the data below showing popular mortgage key phrases vs. real estate key phrases, monthly search volume, and CPC (cost per click) using Google's Keyword Planner Tool:

Mortgage Data:

Keyword (by relevance)	Avg. Monthly searches	Suggested bid
Mortgage Rates San Diego	390	$7.44
VA Loans San Diego	210	$36.54
Mortgage San Diego	170	$10.35
San Diego Home Loans	170	$23.77
Refinance San Diego	30	$29.91

Figure 1-1: average monthly search data for "San Diego mortgage" related key phrases in Google for May 2018.

Real Estate Data:

Keyword (by relevance)	Avg. Monthly searches	Suggested bid
San Diego Real Estate	9,900	$2.07
Homes for Sale in San Diego	8,100	$2.88
San Diego Homes for Sale	4,400	$2.25
San Diego Homes	2,400	$2.50
Condos in San Diego	1,900	$2.00

Figure 1-2: average monthly search data for "San Diego real estate" related key phrases in Google for May 2018.

The numbers play out like this for mortgage vs. real estate online activity in every city of the country.

Search the phrase: "Google keyword planner tool" or go to:

https://adwords.google.com/KeywordPlanner

This is where you can run some tests and see for yourself. I include some additional keywords research tools in Chapter 34.

People are interested in finding their dream home, not a 1003 application. Knowing that gives you a big advantage over your competition when it comes to marketing your mortgage business.

Offering a real estate search tool will allow you to tap into a much larger audience than if you only provide mortgage content on your website.

You can use home search offers that draw people to your website in just about any kind of marketing campaign to drive more traffic.

Examples of such offers include:

"Find your dream home 24/7!"

"Search 1000's of local homes for sale!"

"Find properties eligible for USDA loans!"

"Find properties eligible for 203K loans!"

"Scour our foreclosure database for FREE!"

"Get a list of zero down eligible homes that meet your exact criteria!"

"Get access to exclusive real estate listings you won't find elsewhere!"

Home search offers also work great for specific niches, like: condos, luxury homes, golf course homes, beachfront homes, for sale by owner, pocket listings, expired homes, and much more.

Using real estate searches to generate mortgage leads will help you and your Realtors®, while at the same time turning your website into a "one-stop shop"—keeping borrowers on your website for longer, and giving them more reasons to come back.

Once you've captured their information, your home search tool can simply forward consumers directly to the MLS, or to the listings or home search area of one of your Realtors® websites. You could even pick a different Realtor to feature as your "Agent of the Month" and rotate the home search destination every few weeks.

Home Values Lead Generation Landing Page

Another way to leverage real estate as a strategy for getting additional mortgage leads is to use a home values lead generation landing page.

This will allow you to generate refinance leads for yourself, and home seller leads for your Realtor® partners.

Keep in mind: home sellers today are usually homebuyers tomorrow.

Offering a free home values estimate tool will help you get access to future homebuyers at an early stage of their decision-making process.

More on how to use real estate marketing tactics to your advantage later in the *Manifesto*...

Spoiler alert: it involves partnering with the right Realtors® and having *them* drive traffic for you.

Home Insurance Lead Generation Landing Page

You've seen the phrase "one-stop shop" used a couple times now in this website breakdown... I'm going to continue with that concept.

Your goal is to create a destination for your clients.

You don't want people leaving your website to go out on their own to find other relevant information.

Once they leave, chances are they're not coming back, so keep people on your website for as long as possible and give yourself more reasons to direct clients to use your website.

Here's a fact: the online insurance space is just as bad (if not worse) than the mortgage space when it comes to companies that exist solely to harvest consumer data and sell that information as sales leads.

Clients getting their information sold and then being hounded by relentless insurance salespeople is a crappy situation. That's typically what happens when they start shopping for insurance online.

To help them avoid the hassle, use a home insurance landing page to generate leads that you can share directly with **your select insurance partners.**

Script for Helping Clients with Their Home Insurance

"Hey, so you're going to need to get your home insurance figured out... Do you have someone in mind already?"

*"If not, I recommend you **be careful** when shopping for insurance online, as there are a* <u>ton</u> *of companies out there that'll just sell your information to a dozen or more insurance agents."*

"That means you get multiple calls <u>every day</u> *for the next 2-3 months from insurance agents that bought your information as a 'sales lead'."*

"It's ridiculous, not to mention, a giant pain in the butt."

"Because of that, I've actually created a safe and secure home insurance quote portal for you @ my website, _____.com."

"It only takes about 60 seconds and it will connect you directly with _____, my trusted home insurance pro in the _____ area."

"He/she can give you a competitive quote fast, and if you like the offer, you can get setup right over the phone and computer—that way you have a couple less things to worry about, and you can get this important piece knocked out quickly and easily. The sooner, the better."

"Just go to my website, _____.com, and click on the link that says, 'FREE Home Insurance Quote!'"

You can also email or even text clients a link directly to your home insurance landing page so that they can fill it out right there on their mobile phone!

PLUS—YOU as the mortgage professional referring the client can get paid for home insurance leads, anywhere from $25 to $50 a pop.

Insurance agents pay that much for crappy, used-and- abused internet leads...

Your insurance agent will be stoked to get hooked up with a mortgage partner that feeds them quality, exclusive leads directly.

Not to mention a home insurance policy can easily become a bundled policy for home + auto, and possibly life insurance, especially now that there's a home in the picture (mitigate risk, plan for retirement, and protect the family).

Simply setup an insurance lead generation landing page, find a great insurance partner (or partners), negotiate your payouts, and you're all set!

Depending on how you use this strategy, creating a system for monetizing insurance leads might pay for a nice lunch, or it might pay for an office party...

Either way, it's low-hanging fruit and a passive income strategy that can be completely automated.

Automated Credit Repair System + Lead Generation Landing Page

As a mortgage pro, you're generating poor credit leads and talking to credit-challenged individuals regularly.

Why Not:

► Monetize these leads and get paid every time a credit repair package is purchased (without having to lift a finger)?

► Use an automated system that repairs their credit, tracks everything, and boomerangs leads back to you once their credit qualifies for a mortgage, turning poor credit leads into closed loans?

This is also low-hanging fruit and another passive income strategy that can be completely automated when built into your mortgage website.

All you need is a credit repair landing page to collect information that you can then automatically pass to your trusted credit repair partner.

For more information on credit repair lead monetization, go to:

www.leadPops.com/credit-repair

Mortgage Calculators

Mortgage calculator key phrases are some of the most popular mortgage related key phrases on Google.

People like to play with calculators, but in test after test, calculator related key phrases don't typically convert into leads at a high enough rate to make them profitable.

That's why they're dirt cheap in terms of CPC on Google compared to other mortgage key phrases—from as little as $.30 up to $3.00 per click vs. $8 to $25+ per click for "refinance" and "mortgage rates" based phrases.

Few companies are willing to bid more on them because they're not making money off them.

Like I've said: you can't do business with clicks.

So, I recommend incorporating mortgage calculators into your mortgage website because consumers are looking for them and like to use them in their research, but don't make them the highlight of your website.

Always be sure to showcase your mortgage calculator(s) on a page coupled with a prominent call-to-action button that takes users to a landing page designed to convert leads for something like a custom rate quote. That way you can use calculators as a segue to generate leads instead of just having a bunch of people coming onto your website, fiddling with your calculators, then leaving and you get nothing out of it.

Blog Integration

Blogs are great... if you're committed.

A good blog can help establish you as an authority, get you social followers, comments, shares, repeat traffic, inbound links that can help with search engine placement, and more.

You don't need to be Hemingway, but you've got to know your stuff and you need to be eloquent with solid grammar (and definitely use spell check).

Having a content schedule with 6-12 months of weekly posting topics/articles outlined in advance will help keep you on track and make your blog easier to manage.

On the fly posts as rates fluctuate, new products become available, industry changes are announced, etc. are all great excuses to add to your blog.

If you write pretty well and can commit to 1-2+ new blog posts per week, each with anywhere from 1,000-2,000 words per post (Medium.com says the ideal length of a blog post is 7 minutes, 1,600 words) then definitely get a blog going and make sure you build it into your website to get all the added SEO value.

If you're not a great writer but see the value in a blog, hire a content writing service to pump out 1-2 posts for you each week.

There are several services available to help you find and hire talented content writers. Once you find someone good, you can typically work with that person on an ongoing basis through the service or by connecting with them directly.

Don't skimp on content writers. As with most things, you get what you pay for.

I include a couple content writing services in Chapter 34, so check those out.

Always weave call-to-action links and/or buttons taking readers to lead generation landing pages for related topics into your blog posts to monetize your blog and convert readers into clients.

The *best* way for you to help potential clients is to have a conversation with them, not them anonymously reading your content (no matter how great it is), then leaving and getting sucked into LendingTree's mousetrap (or whoever), all because you didn't optimize your blog content for lead conversion.

That's doing your clients, and you, a disservice.

Social Network Integrations

Make it easy for clients and visitors to share your website with their friends, family, and followers by integrating your social network profiles along with social sharing tools.

Realistically, people don't get all that excited about mortgage websites, but if you include all the tools and features recommended in this chapter, your chances of getting referral traffic and social shares will increase greatly.

Not only can integrating your social profiles help you get more exposure through social networks, but it can also help your search engine rankings.

For cool social sharing tools you can add to any website and much more, go to:

www.AddThis.com (no affiliation to leadPops)

Domain Name

Ideally, you will have a .com domain name (that you own) to use with your mortgage marketing website.

A domain that you're currently driving traffic to, or have marketed in the past, in most cases, will be the best domain to use vs. buying a new domain name, or using a domain that you've had parked for a while but never promoted.

A domain name with some history behind it has a much better chance at placing well in search engines than a new domain.

Not to mention putting a domain name that's already getting traffic on a website that's optimized to convert leads will give you an instant boost in business.

I can't tell you how many times I've seen mortgage pros put a seasoned domain they've been using on a newly conversion-optimized website and go from no leads <u>ever</u> to multiple leads per day, every single day—from the exact same traffic they were getting all along! That's the power of conversion rate optimization.

You can point multiple domains to one website, and even direct various domains to specific pages within your website.

Also, having relevant keywords in your domain name(s) is a good idea.

Secure domains are more expensive to setup and host, but favored by Google, and also add credibility with consumers who are getting savvier about website security, especially when it comes to filling out their personal information.

Use a domain that's short and sweet, easy to spell, memorable, and void of anything cutesy like the number "4" in place of "for" or the letter "u" in place of "you" (unless you own the version with the actual word(s) as well).

If possible, stay away from .net, .co, .biz, .org, etc. You don't want people typing in the .com version (which they will do no matter how much you emphasize the correct extension) and ending up on a competitor's website.

Install Google Analytics

You need to know how much traffic is coming to your mortgage website.

> **Way too many people jump to the conclusion that they get little or no traffic because they get no leads... when in reality, the reason they get no leads is because they have no conversion tools and zero conversion optimization.**

If you have a website, chances are traffic is not your problem, converting traffic into leads is your problem...

And you need to know how big of a problem it is in order to properly evaluate which are your best next steps to take.

Google Analytics provides data on everything you need to know regarding your website traffic, and it's free.

Some of the most important metrics you'll get access to include: number of new visitors, repeat visitors, where they came from, time spent on site, most popular pages, exit pages, and conversion rates.

It's easy to install, and once you understand the interface, you can get all the details you need to know at a glance—uncovering valuable insights as to how your website is performing and where you can improve.

Bonus: for a free guide that will help you hit the ground running with Google Analytics, go to:

www.leadPops.com/manifesto-bonus

How Effective is Your Mortgage Website?

If you're struggling to get results from your website, you're not alone. Most mortgage professionals have pretty much given up on trying to get business from their websites...

It doesn't have to be that way.

Or, if you've got a website that's producing clients for you currently, but you'd like to make it even better, I've got some awesome insight for you as well...

For free, personalized advice on how you can get more business from your mortgage website today, go to:

www.leadPops/website-grader

CHAPTER 2

Launch Multiple High-Conversion Mortgage & Real Estate Landing Pages

It'd be logical for you to assume that the reason I say you should start with launching a mortgage marketing website and multiple landing pages is because my company builds mortgage marketing websites and landing pages.

However, actually, it's the other way around.

The reason we build marketing websites and high-conversion landing pages is because they're the foundation of all your marketing efforts.

If you're trying to generate leads as a loan officer or broker in the mortgage business, this is where you need to start.

Without a website and landing pages that are built to capture and convert qualified leads, you might as well set your marketing budget on fire. No joke.

All too often, mortgage advertising doesn't include a URL option, or just as bad, it's directed at a website homepage that has dozens of unrelated options competing for the attention of the visitor (usually a bunch of stuff to read), or a 1003 application, which, as covered in Chapter 1, is not a lead generator. This results in poor conversions.

That's why your mortgage website needs to have landing pages built into it, and whenever possible, you should be marketing dedicated landing pages as the main destination you drive potential clients to for various marketing campaigns and promotions.

What is a Landing Page?

In online marketing, a landing page is a standalone web page that is detached from your main website and built for a single purpose.

For mortgage and real estate marketing, that purpose is lead generation.

This means the design and content need to be focused on *one business objective*, with <u>one primary call-to-action</u>, and there should be no navigation or menu links taking users to your main website or to other unrelated sites.

The reason for this is to eliminate distractions, keep visitors focused on the objective of the page, and guide them toward your intended goal of converting a lead.

A visitor can arrive on a landing page in a variety of ways, including: after clicking on an offer from a search engine ad (organic or paid), social media campaign, banner, call-to-action link/button in an email, text message, or on a website/blog, a QR code, or by typing in a domain name that points directly to the landing page.

Types of Landing Pages

In the mortgage space, the point of a landing page is typically to convert a click into a quality lead.

There are 2 primary types of landing pages that can help facilitate this objective: "lead generation" (or "lead capture"), and "click-through".

Lead Generation Landing Pages

Lead generation landing pages are used to capture potential client information such as contact info and details regarding their needs.

To qualify as a lead capture page, the landing page must contain a form built into the page, along with a call-to-action and description of what the user will receive for providing their personal info when submitting the form.

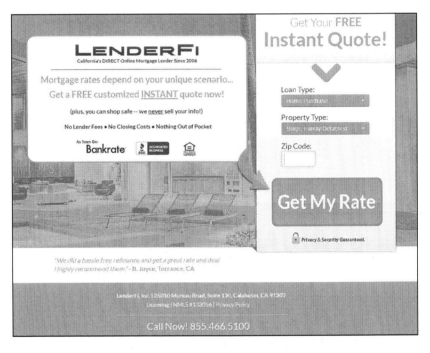

Figure 2-1: example of a high-converting mortgage lead generation landing page.

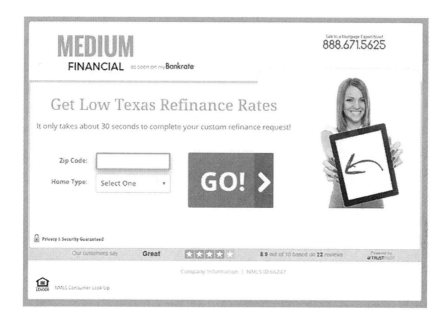

Figure 2-2: one of our top-converting mortgage lead generation landing page designs. Ultra-simple, yet incredibly effective. A/B testing state-specific messaging boosted the conversion rate on this page from 13% to over 17%. That's roughly 40 additional leads for every thousand visits! The "Trust Pilot" strip across the bottom is a simple trust factor and credibility statement. Muy Bueno.

Figure 2-3: another high-conversion mortgage lead generation landing page. You can't help but notice the bright red CTA button moving users into the next step of the form (4-steps total).

Figure 2-4: a sleek lead generation landing page in its mobile state.
The dimensions and components automatically conform to whatever
screen size the user is on, from smartphones to desktop top computers
and everything in between. "Click to Call" automatically appears on
any touch-based device.

Collecting more information on your lead capture page will result in a higher quality lead vs. just collecting a name and email address (which can be great for list building, but not for making immediate sales).

Capturing additional info also means you can better segment your leads for more effective future follow-up campaigns.

To get additional information without overwhelming and scaring potential clients away, you need to break your lead generation form up into multiple steps, and never start out by "going for the jugular"—asking for name, email address, and phone number right off the bat...

I'll cover more on this, and the anatomy of a high-conversion mortgage landing page later in this chapter.

If you're <u>just</u> trying to build your list for future digital marketing, ask for the bare minimum—a name and email address are all you need.

Once you build your list, you can then use email, text messages, Facebook, and/or retargeting to promote a landing page with a more in depth question and answer sequence, which allows you to separate the more serious prospects from the suspects on your list.

Click-Through Landing Pages

As the name suggests, a click-through landing page is one designed to entice visitors to click-through to another related page or web form with the goal of moving them closer to a conversion/sale.

The first page is used as an introductory sales page, with informative content that entices the user and convinces them to click a call-to-action button in order to learn more and/or submit their info.

Figure 2-5: a click-through landing page for VA Loans with a green CTA button above the fold that takes the user to a gamified, multi-step lead generation form, and another CTA button below the fold, also taking the user to the same form.

Figure 2-6: a click-through landing page for refinance with 1 question and 5 CTA buttons as "menu" options to answer the question— "Reason for refinance?"—Lower Monthly Payment, Pay Off Loan Faster, ARM/ Fixed Conversion, Tap Into Home Equity, & Consolidate Debt, as possible answers.

Each CTA button points to a gamified, multi-step lead generation form that matches the message on the CTA button that led to it.

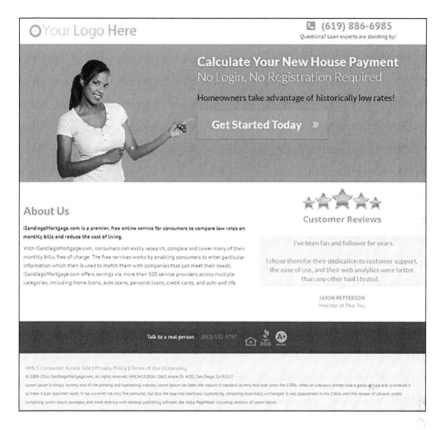

Figure 2-7: a click-through landing page with 1 prominent CTA button taking the user to a gamified, multi-step lead generation form.

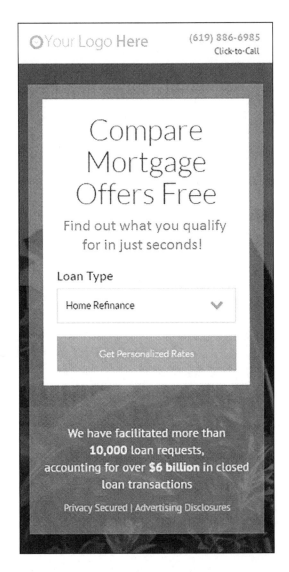

Figure 2-8: a mobile click-through landing page with 1 drop down menu allowing the user to select either refinance or purchase, and 1 prominent CTA button taking the user to a gamified, multi-step lead generation form with questions and messaging based on their answer to that first question.

This act of clicking a non-threatening button without even *seeing* a form or having to fill anything out is a micro commitment that can help get potential clients into the mode of subconsciously saying "yes" to your offer before you start asking for information that can scare them away, like their email address and other contact info.

The destination from a click-through landing page is typically a form or registration page, which will have a much higher chance of conversion as the user has already passed through and "approved" the details on the preliminary click-through page.

It's vital that the click-through page and destination <u>maintain unified design and messaging</u>, otherwise your conversions will suffer.

General Landing Page Purposes

There are countless uses for mortgage and real estate lead generation landing pages. Some examples are listed below:

- ► Consultation or Quote for Professional Services
- ► Contest or Drawing Entry
- ► Discount Coupon, Rebate, or Voucher
- ► Event Registration
- ► Free Report, eBook, Whitepaper, or VIP List
- ► Newsletter Signup
- ► Notification of a Future Product or Service Launch
- ► Physical Gift (sent by mail)
- ► Webinar Registration

B2C Offers for Mortgage Landing Pages

Business-to-consumer (B2C) offers are great for marketing on Google Adwords, Facebook, emails, websites, blogs, banners, directory websites, co-marketing, retargeting, direct mail, radio, television, signage, etc.

- ▶ 15 Year Fixed
- ▶ 203K Loans
- ▶ 30 Year Fixed
- ▶ ARMs
- ▶ Custom Mortgage Rate Quote
- ▶ FHA Loans
- ▶ HARP Loans
- ▶ Home Purchase Qualifier
- ▶ Home Refinance Analysis
- ▶ Jumbo Loans
- ▶ New Construction Loans
- ▶ Reverse Mortgages
- ▶ Today's Mortgage Rates
- ▶ USDA Loans
- ▶ VA Loans
- ▶ Zero Down Financing

B2B Offers for Mortgage Landing Pages

Business-to-business (B2B) offers are great for marketing on LinkedIn, Facebook, emails, websites, blogs, banners, co-marketing, retargeting, direct mail, etc.

- ▶ Recruiting New Realtor® Partners
- ▶ Recruiting New Builders, Attorneys, CPAs, and Other Referral Partners
- ▶ Recruiting Employers for Affinity/Employee Benefits Marketing

B2C Offers for Real Estate Landing Pages

These types of offers are great for marketing on Google Adwords, Facebook, emails, websites, blogs, banners, directory websites, co-marketing, retargeting, direct mail, radio, television, signage, etc.

- ► 203k Eligible Homes
- ► Abandoned Homes
- ► Buyers Guide
- ► Coming Soon Listings
- ► Expired Listings
- ► For Sale by Owner Marketing
- ► Foreclosures
- ► Guaranteed Sale in "X" Days
- ► Home Finder Service—luxury, beachfront, golf course, downtown, condos, etc.
- ► Home Valuation
- ► Inherited Homes
- ► Investor Properties
- ► Neighborhood/School Info
- ► Pocket Listings
- ► Property Reports
- ► Relocation
- ► Sellers Guide
- ► Short Sales
- ► Sold Listings
- ► Vacant Homes
- ► Vacation Homes
- ► VIP Home Search
- ► Zero Down Eligible Listings

There are tons of additional niche topics for mortgage and real estate landing pages and "microsites" covered in Chapter 16.

The more landing pages you have, the better.

If you have 2 landing pages, each converting 10-15 quality leads per month, that's cool... but think if you have 10 landing pages performing at that same rate.

Every marketing campaign should have its own dedicated landing page to ensure high conversions.

Not only do I recommend using landing pages in *your* own marketing efforts, but you can also supply landing pages to partners, like Real Estate agents and builders, for them to use in *their* marketing.

This allows you to share in the leads coming from their campaigns and piggyback off of their marketing efforts.

A great way to convince good Realtors® to want to market you and share in the leads with you is to supply them with badass landing pages that convert quality leads.

They'll have a tough time saying "no" to that, and your competitors will have their work cut out for them when it comes to beating your value proposition.

More on this strategy for partnering with the right Realtors® in Chapter 12.

Introduction to High-Conversion Mortgage Landing Pages

My company, leadPops.com, has been designing and developing mortgage landing pages since 2011.

In 2013, Zillow contracted us for 8 months to help them develop better landing pages and improve conversion rates for their Mortgage Marketplace.

In a matter of weeks, we doubled many of their advertisers' conversion rates, so Zillow turned around and doubled what they were charging for their CPC.

Advertisers weren't too happy about it, but couldn't really object considering their cost per funded loan stayed the same.

I'll get more into conversion rate optimization in Chapter 3, but the formula is: if you double your conversion rate, you can cut your marketing spend in half...

Zillow didn't want their clients spending half, so they jacked up their CPC by double the amount!

That's the power of landing pages and conversion rate optimization...

When done right, you can double your leads, or cut your marketing spend in half, or spend more on marketing and hire some help!

Keep in mind: conversion rates vary depending on a number of factors, including traffic source.

For example: all things considered, a click-through to a landing page from a targeted email blast to a warm list will typically convert much better than cold traffic from a Craigslist ad.

In 2014, Bankrate.com (now one of our partners), hired my company to develop mobile landing pages for their mortgage rate table advertisers.

Because of the success of the mobile landing pages, in 2016 Bankrate added our desktop landing pages to the offer, meaning: Bankrate pays leadPops to develop both desktop and mobile landing pages for all of their new mortgage advertisers.

That's millions of dollars per year in advertising coming through our landing pages—and that's just from Bankrate, who makes up a small portion of our clients.

Bankrate hasn't jacked up pricing on their clients, either.

They're just happy their advertisers are seeing success, and enjoying a higher retention rate and more signups as a result of our partnership.

Over the years, I've had the opportunity to test countless landing page layouts, calls-to-action, colors, questions, visual cues, etc. on tens of millions of borrowers looking to purchase and refinance all over the country.

Currently, leadPops generates between 40,000-50,000 leads per month for clients in the mortgage and real estate industries nationwide.

We get a lot of data out of that.

Many mortgage clients have come to us with landing pages converting at 2-3%.

We work our magic, and often get them up to 10-15% (practically overnight)—and as high as 20-30%.

So what exactly do those numbers mean?

Let's take a landing page that's receiving 1,000 visits per month and give it a decent starting conversion rate of 5%.

That's 50 leads per month.

Bump that up to just 8% and you're at 80 leads per month.

12% and you're at 120 leads per month...

FROM THE EXACT SAME TRAFFIC!

5% conversion on 1,000 visits over 1 year is 600 leads.

12% conversion on 1,000 visits over 1 year is 1,440 leads.

Let me repeat...

FROM THE EXACT SAME TRAFFIC!

Close just 10% of the difference (840) and you've got an extra 84 closed loans.

If you make an average of $3K per loan, that's over $250,000 in commission...

FROM THE EXACT SAME TRAFFIC!

Not to mention your client LTV (lifetime value)—multiple loans and referrals...

Plus the ability to share all these extra leads and referrals with partners, like Realtors®, builders, insurance agents, etc.

Simply put: your conversion rate will make or break the success of your marketing campaigns.

That being said, I know a thing or two about what makes a high-converting mortgage landing page, and I'm going to share a lot of that with you next.

Before I do, I want to mention that several colleagues and friends (including my wife) have asked me if I'm concerned about my competitors getting their hands on this information.

My answer is, "nope".

Why? Competitors have been trying to copy my strategies for the last 12 years and they still can't figure it out. If anything, perhaps this book will help them create better products.

By the time they do, my clients and I will be another 10 steps ahead.

You can't lead from behind when it comes to marketing and technology.

Anatomy of High-Conversion Mortgage Landing Page

Lead Generation vs. Click-through

For most campaigns, you'll want to use a lead generation landing page with a form built right into it.

If your offer is complex and you have more content, like a lot of sales copy or a video that you want to use to educate and entice visitors, you can start with a click-through page that takes users into your lead generation landing page, which should be much simpler and void of a lot of text and other distractions.

In that case, always make sure the messaging and design are aligned to reassure visitors that they've come to the right place.

Desktop & Mobile Landing Pages

Your landing page should be responsive, meaning: the design provides an optimal viewing and interaction experience on everything from desktop computer monitors to smartphones.

There are times where desktop landing pages don't convert leads as well when "morphing" to their mobile state, which may call for a separate landing page for desktop and for mobile, with an auto-detect feature routing users to the correct version depending on what kind of device they're using.

If your landing page is responsive and converts well on desktop but not on mobile (or vice versa), I recommend testing a dedicated version optimized for each experience and seeing how that affects your conversion rates.

Keep in mind, there will always be variances in conversion rates between desktop and mobile traffic. The only way to know if a unique version for each will convert better for any given campaign is to test.

Landing Page Dimensions

Although a well-designed responsive landing page will adjust to any browser/screen size, I still recommend some parameters for the "full sized" version, specifically the content inside the landing page.

Recommended landing page dimensions (starting points):

▶ Width—960px to 1024px

▶ Height—600px to 800px

Users should never have to scroll side to side, and you want to minimize up and down scrolling as much as possible.

Placement of Landing Page Components

The call-to-action, lead capture form, and CTA buttons should all be "above the fold", meaning: you don't have to scroll down to see them.

Less important items, like footer info, compliance text, and trust factor badges (BBB, "as seen on..." etc.) can be placed below the fold if you're struggling with space.

In test after test, I've seen negligible differences in conversion rates whether the form sits on the right side or left side of the landing page.

Empty space is good. You don't want to overwhelm visitors with too much stuff crammed into your landing page competing for attention.

Logo: top left.

Phone number: top right.

Call-To-Action

Your call-to-action is your instruction to your landing page visitors.

Make it concise and focus on the benefit the user will get for submitting their info.

Think, "What's my Unique Selling Proposition?" and get some ideas by taking a look at what the big mortgage lead generation companies are saying with their landing page CTA messaging.

Remember: some of these companies have been testing this stuff for more than a decade, and they're not using messaging that doesn't work.

All it takes is doing a few Google searches for phrases like "CITY refinance" or "CITY mortgage rates" (replace "CITY" with any city or state you're interested in) and click on some of the ads.

Don't feel bad that your click cost them $20 either, they can afford it. That being said, don't click on an ad over and over again either—that's just bad marketing juju.

CTA font should be large, bold, and easy to read. Nothing too fancy, or cursive, or anything like that.

You can support your primary call-to-action with supportive description text or some bullet points, also focusing on the benefits which reinforce the offer in your primary CTA.

Referencing the state and more specifically, city, your traffic is coming from will boost conversion rates vs. just having one catch-all message targeting everyone.

If you're marketing in multiple areas and/or promoting various products, using dedicated landing pages with messaging and imagery geared towards those specific geographic areas, along with language that coincides with the particular loan products and programs you're promoting, will also increase your conversions.

CTA Examples

Purchase—

> **Get Pre-Approved for a San Diego Mortgage**
> It only takes about 30 seconds to complete your custom
> pre-approval request. Start now!

Refinance—

> **Get Low San Diego Refinance Rates**
> You could save thousands of dollars per year on your
> mortgage. That's money in *your* pocket. Start here!

General—

> **Lock in a Low San Diego**
> **Mortgage Rate While They Last**
> Low rates, great service, accurate quotes, and lightning
> fast turnaround time... Get started now!

Gamified Lead Capture Form

Like everything else on this list, it's crucial that you get the lead capture form right.

Great traffic going to a stellar landing page design with an awesome offer and effective messaging will fail if your lead capture form sucks, as most landing page forms do.

Think of your landing page as a vehicle and the form as the engine that powers it. Let's give your engine rocket fuel.

To do that and to get more conversion (leads) out of your form, you need to gamify it.

Badgeville.com defines gamification as, "the concept of applying game mechanics and game design techniques to engage and motivate people to achieve their goals. Gamification taps into the basic desires and needs of the users' impulses which revolve around the idea of status and achievement."

In other words: you want to make filling out your form fun.

Again, and it bears repeating, NEVER start out by going for the jugular—asking for contact information right off the bat. You need to earn that by asking for other, non-threatening information first.

Ask only 1-4 questions at a time and break your form up into multiple steps.

Believe it or not, when done right, forms with more steps and questions often convert better than short forms.

I've seen 5-7+ step forms convert leads at a higher rate than 2-3 step forms time and time again. Not to mention lead quality with more questions answered is much higher.

One-step forms are for amateurs, so don't even talk to me about those ☺.

Start your question and answer process with something easy, like zip code, and then ask a few more qualifying, non-intimidating questions, like:

- ► Loan Type
- ► Home Type
- ► Down Payment
- ► Home Value (ok to estimate)

In total, you want anywhere from 12-24 questions, which will work great if you <u>make it easy for potential clients to answer them</u>.

You accomplish this by not overwhelming people with too many questions at once, and minimizing blank text fields/typing.

That means using drop down menus, yes or no questions, radio buttons, checkboxes, sliders for price ranges, etc.

Eliminate the guesswork by offering predetermined answers as options—think multiple choice quiz vs. fill in the blank... Which would you prefer?

Reduce clicks/taps (time and effort) by presenting menus in an open state instead of making users open menus to make their selections.

Use visual cues, like subtle animations to open/close menus, present questions appearing and disappearing automatically upon answering them, show confirmations like green checkmarks when questions are answered correctly, highlight active blank text fields to draw attention to them, auto-focus the cursor inside active blank text fields so that when users do need to type, the cursor is blinking—ready and waiting for them, use an animated progress meter that zips along as they move through the form to show users a light at the end of the tunnel, enticing them to keep going...

It's a snowball effect—as potential clients answer easy, qualifying questions, they get more and more committed to the process as they go.

Make them feel rewarded and like they're getting somewhere, and they're more likely to keep moving along.

At the end, when you ask for their contact information, it's like the point of no return...

They're a lot more likely to give you that info once they've invested time answering other easy, relevant, non-intrusive questions than they are if contact info is the first thing you ask them for.

You'll also get a much higher rate of <u>real</u> contact information instead of bogus leads like "bart simpson" and "batman" with fake phone numbers, which people are more apt to give you when there's no commitment and they just want to bypass your registration form to see what comes next.

Domain Name

Use a .com domain name that you own, which coincides with the messaging/theme of the landing page.

If it's a landing page for "FHA loans," using a domain name that references "FHA loans" would be prudent.

Security

Secure pages convert better. This means the browser shows "https" in the URL and includes a green lock in the browser bar indicating that the page takes extra security precautions with technology, thus better safeguarding user information.

Setting up a security certificate for your domain name costs a little more, but it's nothing when you consider that it will help you get more leads/close more loans.

Consumers will reward you with their trust by submitting their info at a higher rate because you've taken the extra measure to protect their information with an added level of landing page security.

Colors

Match the landing page design details to the logo and company brand, <u>except</u> for the CTA buttons—make sure those contrast and stand out from the rest of the page.

Phone Number

Be sure to include a phone number on your landing page and make it "click-to-call" for smartphones and tablets.

If you're advertising nationally, use a toll-free phone number. If local, use a phone number with a local area code.

Images & Videos

Your "hero shot" is the featured image (or video) on your landing page.

It needs to help sell your offer and guide people into filling out your form.

My numerous tests have shown that images of a person looking toward and even pointing at or "presenting" the form and CTA button work better than an image of, for example: a smiling family on their porch staring directly back at the landing page visitor.

Also, many tests I've run have shown that females usually convert better than males, and real people work better than cartoons.

Your hero shot should match the target audience you're marketing to and help convey your message.

Ongoing testing of different hero shots for various campaigns is recommended as they can make a big impact on conversions, for better or worse.

Add an arrow image pointing at your lead capture form or CTA button to further help users focus on the most important parts of the page.

Don't use an extravagant background image. You don't want the background to be the highlight of the page, no matter how pretty your picture is.

Tests have shown that background images many times actually hurt conversions as they interfere too much with the most important parts of the page—the CTA messaging, buttons, and lead capture form.

If you're going to use a background image, fade it out or use a color overlay so it doesn't distract users and interfere with your goal of conversion.

Otherwise, using a simple color or texture background works just fine.

Include a security symbol, like a lock icon with a message assuring consumers that their information is kept private and you won't sell their info.

Privacy is important to users and you can emphasize this as other companies that sell leads can't make this claim.

Use trust factor badges, like the BBB logo and "as seen on..." (other credible sites you're advertising on) if you have them.

These should not be too prominent, and don't ever link to these 3rd party websites from your landing page or you'll lose clients as a result.

Always make sure to include an Equal Housing Lender logo (🏠) so that you don't get busted by the compliance police.

Buttons

Your CTA buttons need to stand out and grab your visitors' attention. CTA buttons should be medium to large with contrasting colors, not blending in to match the other design details of your page.

Orange is optimal, also, green, yellow, red, and electric blue work well.

Let me reiterate: if the logo and the rest of the landing page design details are red, don't make the CTA buttons red!

Even if it doesn't look as pretty to you, make them orange or bright blue—something to make them pop off the page and distinguishable.

Instead of button text that says, "Submit" use something like, "Get My FREE Quote!" or "GO!" or "Get Started Now!"

Customer Reviews

1 or 2 short and sweet reviews can also improve your conversion rates.

Use just a quick quote/sentence, not a full blown paragraph as you don't want people getting too distracted.

Remember, the clock's a tickin' and you only have a small window of opportunity to convert visitors into leads.

You don't want them spending that time reading stuff—you want them filling out their information so you can help them!

The full name (or first initial and last name), date of closing, and product type (purchase or refinance) can help add validity to the review(s), which otherwise people often look at as bogus.

A thumbnail image of the reviewer (not a stock photo) can also go a long way in terms of making the review appear more legit—which they should be.

Footer

Your landing page footer is where you want to place your compliance information and business address.

Small font is fine, as long as it's legible. To help with this, avoid serif fonts.

Consolidating compliance info onto outside pages with links going to those pages from your landing page is ideal vs. having a giant wall of text at the bottom of your landing page.

Footer links should open up on <u>top</u> of the landing page in <u>smaller windows</u>, and not redirect users entirely.

This goes for content like: licensing, disclosures, privacy policy, etc.

You can also use lightboxes to link to outside footer content, which would be preferable as those won't link away from the landing page at all.

Lightboxes are windows that open as an extension of the source page, filling the screen and dimming out the rest of the page while keeping the source page in the background (websites like Facebook use lightboxes for photos).

Leakage

Don't link to your website or any other 3rd party websites, especially social media profiles, from your landing page.

That's all unnecessary and an unneeded distraction that will cost you clients.

You want people filling out your form, not clicking onto your Facebook page and getting lost forever.

Thank You Pages Optimization

Your thank you page is the destination your visitors arrive on after submitting their information through your landing page.

Optimizing your thank you pages can help you create a much better, more personalized user experience for your clients, while at the same time improving your call answer and call return rates.

The key is to make your thank you pages rewarding.

Keep your potential clients engaged and absorbed in you and your brand for as long as possible by offering additional value. Don't just shoo away potential clients with an "I'll get back to you later..." message.

Think about it: a brand new prospect or referral has just taken the time to submit a whole bunch of valuable information regarding their wants/needs, along with their personal contact details.

After all that, most landing pages basically just leave people hanging with the promise of a follow-up call in the near future.

That's a golden opportunity right there.

Real quick: make no mistake, I want you to follow-up personally and as fast as humanly possible—that's why my company builds landing pages that provide lead alerts via email and text message, with built-in autoresponders, CRM integrations... You name it.

When you get a new lead, it's critical that you know about it and try to follow-up immediately—we're talking about while people are still looking at the thank you pages message—that's how quick.

However, I also know that, realistically, you're not always able to drop everything and call back a prospect within the ideal window of opportunity, which is 30 seconds or less.

By the way, you think that's fast? Consider this: many large mortgage companies with call center environments have their average call return times down to less than 10 seconds.

So, how do you compete with that?

Well, you can start by offering more value to your customers on your thank you page.

You can personalize their experience and even get a head start on your competition by leveraging technology and automation strategies to guide consumers further along the decision-making and purchase process... without lifting a finger!

There's no way to prevent potential clients from having visited other websites and completing other forms prior to arriving on your landing page and filling out your form, but you can keep them engaged and preoccupied by you and your brand for much longer periods of time once they've found you—especially when they've taken that hugely important step of initiating contact by filling out a multi-step lead capture form—simply by offering exclusive, value-added content on your thank you pages.

Reward potential clients for taking the time to submit their personal information to you by offering content that is only accessible through your thank you pages, upon completing your landing page forms.

Consider mixing and matching any of the following types of content to create a completely customized and rewarding thank you page experience for your potential clients...

- ▶ Affiliate Partner Offers (provide value + get paid for traffic to your thank you pages)
- ▶ Credit Repair Solutions
- ▶ Credit Reporting Tools
- ▶ Customer Reviews
- ▶ Customized Welcome/Intro Video
- ▶ Downloadable PDFs—eBooks, Reports, Whitepapers, etc.
- ▶ Home Insurance Quote Offers
- ▶ Life Insurance Quote Offers
- ▶ Links to Social Profiles (now that you've captured their info, these are OK)
- ▶ Links to Website, Blog, Digital 1003 App, etc.

- ▶ MLS Real Estate Listings—homes for sale, foreclosures, pocket listings, etc.
- ▶ Mortgage Rates
- ▶ Online Calendar / Appointment Scheduling Tool
- ▶ Referral Partner Showcase (featured local Realtor® or builder partner, etc.)
- ▶ Vouchers/Rebates

Make sure the content you offer on your thank you pages matches the audience your landing page and sales copy are geared towards.

If your landing page is promoting free pre-approvals for veterans, make sure the content on your thank you pages is relevant to VA loans and veterans shopping for real estate.

For example: feature a quick 60 second video where you introduce yourself, let viewers know next steps, tell them to check their email for the follow-up information you've sent (autoresponder), and thank them for their service. Include a calendar link allowing them to schedule an appointment right then and there, add below a couple reviews from veterans you've worked with and helped on their mortgage, and below that, a showcase of local services/partners that offer special deals for veterans, like a free or discounted moving truck, savings on bundling home and auto insurance, free pizza, or catered lunch on moving day, etc.

Use a quick call-to-action tagline on the thank you pages encouraging them to bookmark the page and include a link in the autoresponder email taking them back to your thank you pages, allowing them to access the information again at any time without having to go through and fill out your form again.

Keep in mind, a simple thank you message is enough to start out since your primary goals are to generate leads, follow-up quickly, and create personal relationships with your prospects.

However, if you're looking for opportunities to improve your results and you haven't optimized your thank you pages, there's definitely room to grow.

Let me also say that no amount of awesome thank you page optimization can replace the value in your quickly following up with a phone call, building rapport, and all the other wonderful things that happen when you make a personal connection with your potential clients.

CHAPTER 3

Customer Relationship Management (CRM) Software

I f you have a CRM—fantastic, just make sure you're using it consistently and taking advantage of all the most pertinent features.

I also recommend integrating your CRM into all of your marketing to reduce manual data entry and lost leads, while helping you stay on top of sales opportunities.

This includes signup forms on websites, landing pages, and anywhere else online that clients can enter their own contact information to get in touch with you.

If you don't have a CRM, you need to get one ASAP.

A CRM will help you manage leads, contacts, partners, vendors, and more.

You can see everything from background, email history, events, opportunities, etc. With a CRM, you are able to collect and organize data about contacts' behaviors, score them based on interactions, prioritize leads that are hottest, get alerts for follow-ups, automate communication with borrowers, Realtors®, and other partners, and much more.

At leadPops, my team and I have worked with (and done integrations for) just about every mortgage CRM out there.

I know the good, the bad, and the ugly when it comes to functionality and price points.

To make your life easier, here is a list of some of the top CRM companies in the mortgage industry:

- ▶ www.BNTouch.com
- ▶ www.BigPurpleDot.com
- ▶ www.Firepoint.net
- ▶ www.iJungo.com (Salesforce)
- ▶ www.LeadMailbox.com
- ▶ www.MLOshift.com
- ▶ www.MortgageReturns.com
- ▶ www.MortgageIQCRM.com
- ▶ www.Nestablish.com
- ▶ www.TopOfMind.com (Surefire)
- ▶ www.Velocify.com

For a clickable list of links to their websites, go to:

www.leadPops.com/mortgage-crm-list

CHAPTER 4

Complete Marketing CRO Plan—Digital & Traditional Marketing

Digital Marketing

I recommend having all of your digital marketing examined by a conversion rate optimization expert, with CRO consulting for all of your digital marketing, including but not limited to:

► Banner ads

► Blogging efforts

► Email autoresponders & eNewsletters

► Landing pages

► PPC campaigns

► SEO efforts

► Social media

► Videos

► Websites

Traditional Marketing

I also recommend having all of your traditional marketing examined by a conversion rate optimization expert, with CRO consulting for all of your traditional marketing, including but not limited to:

- ▶ Billboards
- ▶ Direct Mail
- ▶ Events
- ▶ Flyers
- ▶ Newspapers
- ▶ Postcards
- ▶ Radio Ads
- ▶ Signage
- ▶ TV Ads

Introduction to Conversion Rate Optimization

As described in Chapter 1, conversion rate optimization is a method for increasing the percentage of users (potential customers) that take a desired action.

The desired action is typically converting from an anonymous potential customer into a tangible contact—a name, email, and phone number.

Keep in mind: the more information you can get, the easier it will be to communicate with and qualify leads.

CRO is a crucial element in marketing because it generates more sales out of the marketing you're already doing.

Here's a key formula to remember about CRO:

Double your conversion rates and you cut your CPA (cost per acquisition) in half.

That means if you spend $1,000 to close 2 loans, doubling your conversion rate gets you 4 loans for that same $1,000 spend.

In other words: you pay $250 to close a deal instead of $500.

To make more sales from your marketing efforts, you can do two things—

1. Spend more money on marketing and hope more leads and sales result from it.

2. Focus on the effectiveness of your marketing by testing, tweaking, and fine-tuning it to get more business out of the marketing dollars you're already investing.

For the same reason you wouldn't pour water into a bucket that's full of holes, you don't want to do any marketing without first optimizing to convert opportunities into customers at the highest rate possible.

Marketing without optimizing to convert leads is literally throwing money out the window.

When's the last time you sold a mortgage to a click?

The good news is that in many cases, getting better results through conversion rate optimization doesn't mean a total overhaul of your marketing.

You can often see drastic improvements from relatively simple changes.

The beauty of CRO is it helps you take advantage of low-hanging fruit—and the opportunities to increase leads and sales are usually much more abundant than you think.

Understanding where to start and what to test can be difficult for those new to CRO, so I'll make it easy.

One of the most basic CRO questions that you can ask is, "What am I trying to get people to do here?"

Let's use a mortgage website as an example...

Is the goal for people to—

- ▶ Read a bunch of stuff?
- ▶ Play with my calculators?
- ▶ Fill out my application?

If the ultimate goal is to make sales—people reading stuff, playing with calculators, and a loan application—aren't going to do the trick. At least not by themselves.

Content is good for educating people, but if you haven't optimized the content to drive visitors into effective lead generation tools (landing pages), and people are just skimming through it and bouncing, what good is it?

Same with calculators; even fancy ones with charts and graphs. They might be fun to play with, but without CRO, what's the benefit of someone you're never going to speak to playing with your mortgage calculator?

How about a loan application?

Think about it: do people you've never spoken with typically just jump into a 1003 on their own?

How often do you receive a totally random, completed online loan application out of the blue?

Referrals aren't a slam dunk, either, so you need to have tools and systems in place that automatically engage these potential clients and help them transition from an anonymous viewer of a marketing piece, or online click, into a conversation.

The purpose of CRO is to evaluate your marketing efforts and come up with tests to implement in order to increase conversion rates/ leads.

Meaningful improvements to your conversion rates can come from the most basic changes.

Here are several tests/ideas that are easy to implement and can help boost your sales pipeline quickly:

- ► Implement call-to-action (CTA) headlines on your website homepage and subpages
- ► Use CTA buttons to drive consumers into lead generation landing pages and engagement tools like live chat and online calendar appointment scheduling tools
- ► Use arrows pointing to CTA buttons and offers
- ► Placement of CTA headlines, buttons, and offers—make them prominent by positioning them "above the fold" and throughout your content
- ► Use guarantees
- ► Enhance your sales copy
- ► Test copy length—sometimes longer works better and vice versa
- ► Change form fields from fill-in-the-blanks to drop down menus, radio buttons, and sliders so users can point and click/tap instead of having to type
- ► Ask for contact information last on your forms, not first
- ► Add reviews with images instead of just text
- ► Improve the layout and design of your marketing pieces—always include a CTA and web address
- ► Test different images
- ► Remove unnecessary menu items and navigation from pages
- ► Remove clutter and useless content
- ► Change button color—use contrasting colors to make buttons stand out instead of blending in

- ▶ Change button CTA text—try testing first person and second person copy ("Get your free quote!" vs. "Get my free quote!")
- ▶ Offer bonuses like free eBooks, complimentary consultations, credit evaluations, discounts on mortgage related services, etc.
- ▶ Replace industry jargon with plain English that non-mortgage people will understand

Take a look at what the biggest, most successful companies in the mortgage and real estate industries are doing with their websites, marketing, landing pages, banner ads, emails, etc. to get an idea of what's working and what isn't. Once again, there's no reason to reinvent the wheel.

Here's a search engine that shows you display/banner ad creatives and ad copy for just about any company running ads online:

www.Moat.com

Once there, search for the following companies to see the ads being run by some of the big dogs in the mortgage and real estate industries:

- ▶ Guaranteed Rate
- ▶ LendingTree
- ▶ LowerMyBills
- ▶ Quicken Loans
- ▶ Ratemarketplace
- ▶ Rocket Mortgage
- ▶ Trulia
- ▶ Veterans United Home Loans
- ▶ Zillow

Researching ad campaigns of marketing juggernauts is an excellent way to get an idea of what the biggest companies out there are doing with their CTA messaging, banners, headlines, offers, color schemes, button copy, etc.

They've spent a lot of money and time testing these ads, and that site will show you exactly what they're running, so use *their* research to *your* advantage.

Keep in mind: I share many more marketing tools in Chapter 34, so there's plenty more for you to draw from. Feel free to do so liberally!

Bottom line: once you implement conversion rate optimization into your marketing efforts, you'll truly know what's working and what isn't, allowing you to scale your successful campaigns for maximum ROI and eliminate stuff that's not profitable.

Until you do, you're missing out on opportunities that are right in front of you.

Using Calls-to-Action to Get More Leads

A call-to-action, or CTA, is an instruction designed to provoke an immediate response and persuade your audience to take action.

Calls-to-action should be integrated into all of your marketing efforts, both online and offline.

When marketing a service or product, you need to give consumers specific direction. You can't assume people will know what to do on their own. That's where a strong CTA comes into play.

Verbiage, font types, font sizes, colors, text placement, and imagery all have an impact on the effectiveness of your calls-to-action and should be tested.

Some CTA guidelines include:

1. **Make your call-to-action clearly visible.**

    The goal of marketing is to get consumers to respond, so you need to make sure the CTA and offer don't get lost in the shuffle.

With websites, landing pages, emails, etc., always position your main CTA above the fold, meaning, positioned in the upper half of the webpage so it's visible without scrolling down the page.

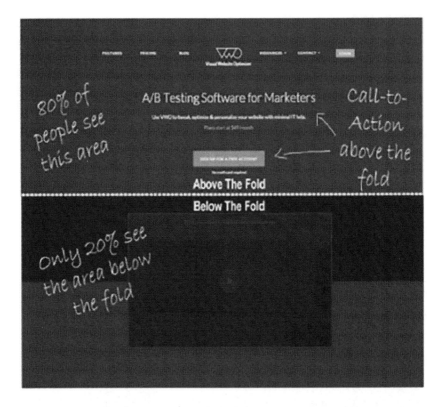

Figure 4-1: a website showing the call-to-action headline and CTA button above the fold.

Consumer engagement usually peaks while visitors are above the fold, so by placing important elements such as your main headline, form, and call-to-action buttons at the top of the page, you'll increase the rate at which your potential clients take action.

If your page has a lot content and scrolls down a bit, include additional CTA buttons below the fold as well.

With offline marketing such as mailers, flyers, publication ads, etc.—also make sure your headline and call-to-action/offer are prominent, ideally at the top of the page and not hidden in the rest of the content.

To maximize response rates on offline marketing, always couple your CTA with a web address that drives potential clients to a lead generation landing page (or website) that's designed to convert leads.

Remember: these days, consumers don't like to just pick up the phone and call salespeople. They want to do their research and remain anonymous for as long as possible.

I know you would prefer a phone call, but unfortunately, people don't care about what you want.

That's why a good call-to-action directing potential clients to a web address with a page that's designed to convert leads will get you a much higher ROI on your offline advertising efforts than if you just promote a phone number.

2. **Use a call-to-action button to guide people into your lead capture forms or other engagement tools.**

    People surfing the web look for buttons, so creating CTA buttons with a contrasting color schemes that stand out can help you get more leads, if that CTA button drives people to a good landing page, form, or some sort of other engagement tool, like a lead magnet, live chat, or online appointment scheduling tool.

Figure 4-2: a banner ad example with a prominent CTA button.

If your advertisement is offline and doesn't allow for a CTA button, make sure that the CTA text is larger and bolder than the rest of the ad copy so that it stands out.

Bonus: to download 700+ mortgage and real estate call-to-action buttons that you can use on your website, blog, email blasts, banner ads, etc. for free, go to:

www.leadPops.com/manifesto-bonus

3. **Make the call-to-action concise.**

When it comes to making an offer with a call-to-action, you need to convey your point as quickly and clearly as possible.

Attention spans are very short, especially online, so if you don't make your point quickly, you risk potential clients missing (or ignoring) your CTA.

For example: if your goal is to drive traffic to a landing page, make sure the language you're using supports that objective.

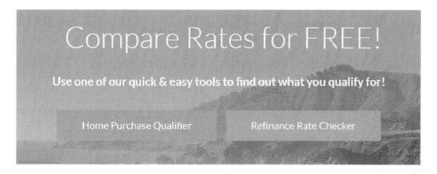

Figure 4-3: snapshot of a mortgage website homepage offering a clear, concise primary CTA headline along with a supportive secondary headline guiding users to 2 call-to-action buttons—1 for each type of borrower, purchase and refinance.

Incentivize consumers by focusing on what's in it for them.

Also, be sure to always deliver on your offer by driving potential clients to a destination that directly coincides with your CTA.

This is called maintaining a consistent "ad-scent" or "message match", which I'll be getting into more shortly.

4. **Add a sense of urgency to your call-to-action.**

Make it clear in your copy that the offer won't be available forever.

Let them know "now" is that time to act, because for you—"later" really means "never".

Figure 4-4: banner with a strong refinance CTA urging potential clients to take action on an offer that won't be around for long.

You can boost your response rates simply adding an imperative verb, for example: "Start Saving Now", which often results in higher click-throughs and conversions.

Using time-sensitive language like "Last Chance" or "Only 24 Hours Left," along with a deadline can also make a big difference.

Boost Conversions with Consistent Ad-Scent

In marketing, a consistent "ad-scent", also known as "message match", means maintaining a connection between your offer (call-to-action in a banner, email, blog post, etc.) and your destination page (landing page or website).

Strong ad-scent ensures that visitors reach your destination page and find exactly what they expect, which can increase conversions dramatically.

Consumers follow items of interest in their web searches similar to animals tracking scent in their search for food—if the scent is strong, they'll stay on the trail...

If they lose the scent, they'll quickly lose interest and head elsewhere. The same idea applies in marketing.

When it comes to your campaigns—emails, banner ads, pay-per-click, retargeting, social media posts, direct mail, radio ads, signage, etc.—always keep the ad-scent aligned from start to finish.

To accomplish this, pay attention to three main components when putting together your ad:

- ► Design
- ► Benefit
- ► Offer

Let's break these down individually so you have a better idea how to implement each aspect in your campaigns.

The Design

When creating your ad and destination page, be sure to keep the design cohesive.

Taking consumers to a destination that matches the ad they clicked or the mailer they received reminds people they've arrived where they intended.

Things to keep in mind while developing your campaign:

- ► Keep your ad colors the same as those on your destination page.

▶ Keep the layout of your ad similar to that of the destination page.

▶ If you're using imagery in your ad, keep it similar (if not exactly the same) as imagery on your destination page.

▶ Make sure the font styling and coloring are the same on both the ad and the destination page.

The Benefit

Why should consumers click your ad? What are they going to get out of it?

A click on your ad means there was interest in your offer, so the content on the destination page should be consistent with the ad.

Take a look at this display ad from the PPC gurus at WordStream. com:

Figure 4-5: the banner on the left works well with the destination landing page on the right, offering a matching design, benefit, and offer.

The banner ad does a great job piquing interest, focusing on the main benefit—"what's in it for you"—in this case, a free guide.

They do an excellent job of making it prominent on both the ad and destination page, while keeping a consistent headline, imagery, messaging, and colors.

When developing your campaign benefits:

- Include text in your ad outlining the major benefit(s) for the consumer, and be sure to include those benefits on the destination page.
- Always focus on, "What's in it for them?" when crafting your benefits.

The Offer

Your offer is the most important part of your ad. It's the ultimate reason people will convert, so make sure to:

- Use the exact same language you used in your ad to get the click in the first place.
- Make your offer clear and use call-to-action language directing potential clients where and how to take action.

To summarize: ALL of your marketing needs to be optimized for conversion.

There are many simple tests/updates you can implement that can have big results on your bottom line, so don't just spend more money on advertising without first optimizing your current efforts to get the best results possible.

You might find that you can squeeze more than enough business out of your current ad spend and efforts by improving your conversion rates instead of just spending more money on marketing.

CHAPTER 5

Monthly e-Newsletter & Email Marketing CRO

When it comes to marketing, an email has the ability to reach a huge audience faster and cheaper than just about anything else.

The average working adult checks their email over 100 times per day.

A well-executed email campaign can entice consumers to take action, convert them into customers, and eventually repeat clients and referrals.

Optimizing Your Emails in 6 Simple Steps

Step 1: Use a clever and engaging subject line.

The subject line is your opportunity to make your email stand out from the dozens, possibly hundreds, of emails your recipients are getting daily.

A few different types of subject lines that work well are those that:

- ▶ Are funny or shocking
- ▶ Are mysterious
- ▶ Are personalized
- ▶ Create curiosity

- ► Create urgency
- ► Use a call-to-action
- ► Use a single word
- ► Use numbers and lists

Make sure that if you boast a claim or imply something in your subject line to increase open rates, you deliver content relevant to that promise inside the email.

Also, keep your subject lines under 50 characters—you'll get higher open rates and your subject lines won't get cut off.

Step 2: Keep it simple and use plain text, not just design templates.

Fancy emails with headers, graphics, and videos can be great for one-off promotions and monthly newsletters, but they're not ideal for every email correspondence you send.

You don't want to overload all of your emails with too much HTML or a lot of images—those are more likely to trigger spam filters.

Your email recipients are just regular people, and the more human you come across in your emails, the better. On that note, stay away from industry jargon and over-the-top professional language.

If you're using email autoresponder software, be sure to customize those emails. You don't want your automated emails to come across as spammy and robotic.

Plain text is ideal for autoresponders so they appear as if you sent them personally, making it more likely for them to get replies. The goal isn't to trick people; it's to effectively automate mundane procedures so you can focus on the important things which cannot be automated.

Step 3: Be concise, provide value, and use calls-to-action.

Again, simplicity is key. Make it easy for your readers to understand the point of your emails.

Don't just send them a wall of text, and be sure to space your paragraphs in such a way that makes your message easy to digest.

Direct your readers with calls-to-action that move them toward the desired goal, whether it's clicking a link to a landing page, filling out a loan application, entering a contest, referring a friend, calling in, etc.

For example: if you're sending out an email blast regarding refinancing—direct your readers to find out how much they can save each month by using your "free 60-second refinance analysis tool", (a refinance-specific landing page or lead capture form).

Step 4: Create clickable links within your email campaigns that take recipients to your landing pages.

If you have an e-newsletter and/or email marketing system, dynamic landing pages and CRO need to be integrated into your campaigns.

Past clients and subscribers aren't necessarily just going to call you or jump into your 1003 application because you've done a good job of staying in front of them with an email campaign.

Along with providing your recipients with the direction you want them to take, make it simple for them to know where to click.

Include call-to-action buttons and/or text links related to your email subject that drive recipients to the next destination—ideally, a landing page with content and messaging that corresponds to the content of the email.

This is the proactive way of helping your subscribers cross the chasm from email recipients to conversations, and then closed loans.

Step 5: Use a landing page with a gamified "smart" form to collect additional info.

I will repeat: you can't expect people to pick up the phone and call you as a result of an email you sent them.

I know you want the phone to ring—in a perfect world, that would happen every time.

However, in today's market, if you're not channeling your email recipients to a dedicated landing page, you're missing out on opportunities left and right.

Keep in mind, leads in your database need to be rekindled.

Just because they're on your list and you email them from time to time doesn't automatically equate to business.

The goal is to separate the serious potential sales from the rest, and convert them from an email recipient/click into a conversation.

You accomplish this by tying a dedicated landing page into your email with clickable links and/or call-to-action buttons that drive them off of the email and into your engagement tool—ideally, a landing page that's relevant to the topic of the email (message match) with a "smart" form built in.

A smart form doesn't just ask for contact information.

Rather, it asks qualifying questions in a friendly, non-intimidating, easy-to-answer way that helps you gauge the quality of the lead and better prepare for the follow-up call.

Landing pages and forms are covered in detail in Chapter 2.

Step 6: Automate your follow-up with autoresponders.

The more you automate your follow-up, the more time you'll have for more important things—like closing loans and spending time with loved ones.

Integrate your lead generation tools—landing pages, website forms, lead magnets, etc.—with your email software so that any leads that come in drop right into your email marketing automation system.

From there, you should be able to track open rates, responses, send automatic replies, segment recipients into different categories, and much more.

This alone can save you hours of data entry throughout the year.

For more on email marketing automation, go to:

www.leadPops.com/email-fire

Email Marketing Piece Analysis—BEFORE and AFTER + SUMMARY

The following is an example of an email marketing piece one my clients sent me a recently for feedback.

The "before" version is very typical of the content sent out by many automated email marketing systems in the mortgage industry—lots of fluff with little to no focus on "what's in it for them", practically no call-to-action, and zero conversion optimization, meaning: unless recipients reply to the email or call the number at the bottom, there's no way to convert them into an active lead in your pipeline.

The "after" version addresses these issues and shows how simply adding a few links to the content of the email brings it to life, and helps take the recipient from just a reader, to a potential client that's interacting and answering questions about their loan scenario.

Before:

ORIGINAL:

   SUBJECT --

   Let's Discuss Your Mortgage Options

Partner with a Strong, Experienced Lender

Kyle,

████████████████████ and I provide our clients experience, financial stability and complete access to the best mortgage products available in the industry. In this sometimes volatile market, it pays to partner with a professional.

I would like to schedule a time for us to discuss your current mortgage. If your financial situation has changed or you have a new loan, I would be happy to review either for savings opportunities.

████████████████████ and I appreciate your business. Please contact me at ███████████ or ████████████████████████to review your loan or to discuss how we might lower your monthly payment.

Sincerely,

███████████████

Figure 5-1: this is the original email the loan officer was sending to his clients, offering no value and focusing on "me, me, me".

After:

REVISED:

SUBJECT --

[Mortgage Quiz] That Can Save You Thousands!

~~Partner with a Strong, Experienced Lender~~

Hi Kyle,

Time is money, so I'll make this quick :)

I've created a free online "mortgage quiz" to help you determine how much you can save on a home purchase or refinance with my team.

It only takes about 60 seconds and you'll get personalized results without any obligation.

Simply click here to get started and find out how much you can save on your mortgage now

If you'd prefer to speak with me directly, please contact me at ▓▓▓▓▓▓▓ or simply reply to this email to discuss how we can help you lock in a low monthly payment today.

Sincerely,

P.S. -- If you know someone that needs help with their mortgage, please feel free to share my information with them.

For each referral you make that closes their loan with me, I'll make a donation of $50 to the charity of your choice. Don't hesitate to forward this email to your family and friends!

Start My FREE Mortgage Quiz

Figure 5-2: this is the revised version of the email with a focus on "what's in it for them", along with calls-to-action and clickable text links taking readers to interactive landing pages.

Revisions Summary & Feedback

1. Focus on what's in it for them—not how great you and your company are.

2. Blue underlined text shows where you'd embed clickable links driving your readers to your landing page.

3. Call-to-action links are crucial in getting the most out of email campaigns.

4. In this scenario (since the email content caters to both purchase and refi), you'd drive recipients to a custom rate quote landing page for conventional loans.

5. If your content is focused on just one specific topic—purchase or refi, or jumbo, or VA, or 203K, or whatever it is you're promoting—then you want to drive them to a landing page that caters to that specific topic/niche.

6. Once again, maintaining a consistent ad-scent ensures visitors to your landing page get exactly what they expect to find, which will increase your conversion rates.

7. Use a "PS"—those stand out and always tend to get read, even if readers skip through the body content of your email.

   A PS can reiterate your primary call-to-action, offer a bonus, testimonial, personalized note or message, or other value-added content/info.

This is the kind of stuff you want to incorporate into pretty much all of your email sequences.

Obviously, if it's a brand new lead and you already JUST collected their info, it doesn't make sense to drive them back to a landing page that asks for the same information again.

However, anything that's even a few weeks old or more can be driven right back to a landing page.

You may have a new offer, rates may have changed, their credit scenario might not be the same, new loan programs or options may be available, etc.

CHAPTER 6

Use a Branded Email Account That YOU Own

If you're still using an email address for your business that ends with something like—@gmail.com, @hotmail.com, @aol.com, etc.—it's time to drop that and get a professional branded email @ your own domain name.

Same goes for emails that end with @ [your-company-domain]. com (if you don't own the company).

It's not good business practice to brand everything with, and send every correspondence through, an email that's at a domain name that doesn't belong to you.

You want your email address to be branded with a domain name YOU own so that it goes where you go.

Mortgage professionals change companies often. Starting over with a new email address every time you change companies over the life of your career will result in a ton of lost business.

You can always forward your old email account(s) to your new one so you do not have to check two emails.

Pick a domain, then setup Gmail for Business. It's a great option for using your own branded email account, and you can get the link to set one up here (no affiliation to leadPops):

www.leadPops.com/pro-email

CHAPTER 7

Brand YOU, Not Just Your Company Name & Logo

This goes hand-in-hand with using your own email address at a domain name that you own.

You don't want to promote your company's logo and name on everything without promoting YOU (if you can do anything about it).

Sure, your company loves that, but it's not good business for you personally...

Marketing your company first and foremost causes you to lose clients and referrals that should be coming to you, but end up going to other LOs in your company instead.

If your company allows you to use a DBA ("doing business as"), awesome—do that. Pick a business name and logo you can be proud of, and use it as a long as you're in the industry and with a company that allows DBAs.

Here are some resources for setting up your DBA and getting custom logos designed (no affiliation to leadPops):

- ▶ www.GoDaddy.com—Domain Registrar
- ▶ www.LegalZoom.com—DBA Service
- ▶ www.LogoDesignGuru.com—Logo Design Service
- ▶ www.ZillionDesigns.com—Logo Design Service

If you can't setup a DBA because your company doesn't allow it, always be sure to promote your name and photo so that people remember you, not just your company.

Of course, the quality of your work and service have a huge impact on whether or not you'll get repeat business and referrals, but if you fail to market yourself correctly, you will miss out on clients regardless of how great of a job you do on the loan.

People don't call to report to you that they went with somebody else, either, so focus on building your brand and you'll have one less thing to worry about.

CHAPTER 8
Facebook Growth Strategies

Prior to 2013, most advertising experts felt that Facebook was a fun social website for sharing pictures and connecting with friends, but had little commercial value as a profitable advertising platform.

Things changed in 2013, when Facebook developed partnerships with giant data brokers like Acxiom, Datalogix, and Epsilon.

Acxiom alone claims to have information on half a billion active consumers globally, with, on average, 1,500 data points per person in their system.

Combined, the databases of these 3 companies collect <u>trillions</u> of data transactions each year.

That means Facebook knows a lot more about you than what you voluntarily provide in your profile description...

Just paid off your car? Currently renting but looking to buy? Graduated from college with your Master's and recently got a promotion?

You guessed it: Facebook most likely knows all of that, and a whole lot more...

Which, likely sounds a little creepy, but if you look at it as a marketer, it's a goldmine.

Facebook gives you the power to target customized audiences beyond your wildest imagination (which we'll get into in a bit), and if you couple that with the right kinds of ads, which are made up of good offers pointing to landing pages that convert leads, you can use Facebook as a medium to consistently close loans.

The Basics

Let's be real: people don't really get excited about the mortgage business. Clearly, I do, as this book indicates, but I'm kind of a weirdo like that.

I'm pretty sure you do, too, or else you wouldn't be reading this...

But most normal people don't.

Understanding that will go a long way in helping you get more loans each month.

As a mortgage pro, you can get a ton of business from Facebook, but you need to approach it from the right angle.

That starts with understanding the kinds of offers people will be more likely to respond to.

As mentioned in earlier chapters, there's a lot more interest in real estate than in mortgage.

Google data showing 5-100X more searches for real estate related key phrases vs. anything mortgage related tells you where the action is at in terms of peoples' interests.

That means advertising real estate listings, homes for sale, exclusive property lists, property reports, market reports, home values, foreclosure deals, short sales, home grants, open houses, zero down programs and homes eligible for zero down financing, homes eligible for 203K loans, homes eligible for USDA loans, and other niche, real estate related offers will get you a lot more clicks and leads than trying to advertise straight mortgage offers.

Growing your fans on Facebook as a mortgage professional can be tough if you go about it the wrong way, but if you use the strategies outlined in this chapter, you can get a respectable Facebook following, while building your reviews and online reputation.

That will establish you as a local market expert, increase your credibility, keep you in front of past clients and referral partners, position you to generate leads for your Realtors® and other referral partners, and ultimately, help you close more loans.

Facebook Engagement

Generally speaking, the more quality Facebook fans you have, the better.

Facebook "fans" are not the same as Facebook "friends", and if you don't have a Facebook business account setup yet, that's going to be your first step.

Bonus: If you're new to Facebook for business, get advice on starting out here:

www.leadPops.com/manifesto-bonus

You can setup a primary Facebook page for your mortgage business, plus additional "Community" pages for your real estate marketing efforts.

Examples include pages like: "Buying in CITY" or "CITY Home Values" or even a "Living in CITY" page, none of which would be branded with a mortgage company, instead would be focused on local community info, events, real estate, etc.

Fans are people that "like" your page, which can be clients, business partners, friends, family, and even leads/potential clients you've interacted with that didn't end up doing business with you.

The best way to grow your fans organically is by consistently posting a variety of engaging, relevant, and helpful content, including but not limited to: articles, videos, lead magnets, images, stories, infographics, quizzes, surveys, cool deals/coupons/rebates, etc.

You can also pay to have posts "boosted", which enables you to reach a much larger audience at a relatively low cost.

Boosting posts will increase your exposure and often get you more likes and fans, assuming the content you're promoting has value.

You want to encourage your audience to interact with your posts by asking questions, and for feedback and comments.

Be sure to respond to any and all interactions to your posts.

The more people interact with your page, the better chance you'll have at showing up in their news feed later on.

Keep in mind: even if your main goal is to generate leads, do not make every update a sales pitch (follow the 80/20 rule, or even 90/10—value/sales), and don't just post mortgage stuff—that's boring.

If you're sharing 3rd party websites, be conscious of the types of content and ads that are regularly featured on that website... staying away from offensive stuff is obvious, but what might not be so obvious is that there are mortgage ads all over many mainstream websites.

I often see mortgage pros posting content that takes consumers to websites of competitors (like Zillow—don't post links to Zillow, they don't need any more of your help!), or sites that are loaded up with ads for companies like LendingTree, LowerMyBills, QuickenLoans, and other mortgage lead vultures...

You obviously can't always avoid websites that *might* show mortgage ads, but some sites are definitely worse than others when it comes to featuring your competition, so check them out before just linking to them for an article on home décor or whatever it might be.

Also, note that if you've been on one of these mega mortgage websites lately, you're probably getting retargeted, so you may be seeing their ads all over the place, but that's not necessarily what everyone else is seeing... Just something to consider.

If you want to clear your browser of all the companies that are retargeting you, Google has a simple guide to clearing cookies in their support for Chrome and other browsers:

www.leadPops.com/clear-cookies

Warning, this will also clear your passwords and other stuff, so tread lightly if you're unsure of what you're doing.

Back to Facebook...

Use hashtags (#) in front of keywords, like:

- ▶ #203k
- ▶ #AnotherLoanClosed
- ▶ #BuyWithZeroDown
- ▶ #(CITY) (i.e.— #SanDiego)
- ▶ #(CITY) Homes (i.e.— #SanDiegoHomes)
- ▶ #(CITY) HomesForSale (i.e.— #SanDiegoHomesForSale)
- ▶ #(CITY) RealEstate (i.e.— #SanDiegoRealEstate)
- ▶ #(CITY) Realtor (i.e.— #SanDiegoRealtor)

- ▶ #FHALoan
- ▶ #Homebuyers
- ▶ #HomesForSale
- ▶ #HomesForVeterans
- ▶ #HomesForHeroes
- ▶ #HomeGrants
- ▶ #HomeLoans
- ▶ #HomePrices
- ▶ #HomeValues
- ▶ #HotPropertyList
- ▶ #LowerMonthlyPayments
- ▶ #Mortgage
- ▶ #MortgageSavings
- ▶ #PropertyList
- ▶ #OpenHouse
- ▶ #RealEstate
- ▶ #Refinance
- ▶ #SaveOnYourMortgage
- ▶ #SaveWith203k
- ▶ #SaveWithUSDA
- ▶ #Savings
- ▶ #USDA
- ▶ #VALoan
- ▶ #VALender
- ▶ #Veterans
- ▶ #ZeroDown
- ▶ #ZeroDownHomes

- ▶ #ZeroDownLoans
- ▶ #ZeroDownMortgage

These hashtags can help your content get picked up by users on Facebook searching for similar content to that of your post.

Another great strategy for Facebook and Instagram (which is owned by Facebook) is to take photos of you with your clients at closing—at your office signing the final documents, or in front of their new home with a sold sign, cutting a ribbon, and/or something awesome like a quality gift—good wine or a gift basket.

Separate yourself from 99.9% of the loan officers out there by getting some props you can reuse again and again, like a "Sold!" sign, and have clients hold the sign and gift in the photo.

This might seem cheesy but who cares? It's awesome and clients will almost always go along with it.

You can post these images to Facebook and Instagram, and "tag" your clients by using "@" in front of their Facebook name/handle to get added exposure to all of their friends and family. This will get your post onto *their* timeline.

Of course ask for permission, but remember: most people are thrilled about their new home purchase, or the hundreds of dollars you saved them with a refinance, and will be more than happy to post the news onto their Facebook timeline and Instagram to share with family and friends.

If a Realtor® or builder is involved in a transaction and does a great job, tag them as well.

This is not just a cool thing to do as it gets them more exposure, but also allows you to ride on their coattails since your post will be shared with their followers and on their timeline as well.

Boosting these posts will give you the perfect opportunity to link up to a landing page/funnel, using calls-to-action offering viewers to:

- ► Get Pre-Approved Now
- ► Get a Home for ZERO Down
- ► Find Out If YOU Qualify
- ► See How Much YOU Can Save
- ► See How Much YOU Can Get
- ► Search Local Homes Now
- ► Find Your Home's Value
- ► Find Down Payment Assistance Programs
- ► Get a Detailed Property History Report
- ► Get a List of Foreclosures in YOUR Area
- ► Get an Exclusive List of Zero Down Eligible Homes
- ► Get Instant Access to "Just Reduced" Properties
- ► Get Instant Access to This Week's New Listings
- ► Get Instant Access to USDA Eligible Homes
- ► Get Instant Access to Homes Just Like This
- ► Get a List of Foreclosures in YOUR Area
- ► Get a FREE Refinance Analysis

… and countless other similar calls-to-action (depending on the content of the post), which would be followed by a clickable link that drives viewers directly to a lead generation landing page with content and messaging that also reflects that of the post.

For longer posts that contain CTA links, be sure to place the link before Facebook truncates the text with "see more", usually at about 400-500 characters.

This way, your viewers won't have to click "see more" to access your call-to-action and landing page.

Best times to post on Facebook based on 2016 data collected by CoSchedule.com:

- ► Saturdays & Sundays, 12:00 PM - 1:00 PM
- ► Wednesdays, 3:00 PM - 4:00 PM
- ► Thursdays & Fridays, 1:00 PM - 4:00 PM

Facebook Ads

Facebook ads are a great channel for generating exclusive leads, typically at a much lower cost per click than Google Adwords.

The number of users as of August 2016 (1.65 billion), and the average amount of time they spend on Facebook daily (50 minutes), make it a tool every mortgage professional should consider using to grow their business.

A major difference between Google PPC (pay per click) and Facebook ads (PPC or impression, depending on the campaign objective) is that with Google, consumers are actually searching for your services using keywords that you're targeting, whereas with Facebook, you're targeting people based on demographics, behaviors, and interests (people that aren't necessarily looking for you).

That means it *might* take more clicks to convert a qualified lead since people on Facebook (sometimes) just click on ads that look catchy/interesting, or out of boredom because an ad appeared on their screen, not because they were proactively searching for, or genuinely interested in, that product or service.

All things considered, Facebook advertising can work very well to generate exclusive mortgage leads… if you approach it right, using the same strategies I shared earlier in this chapter regarding posting and engagement.

That means you should focus much more on real estate than mortgage, and on driving traffic from Facebook to responsive lead generation landing pages.

Facebook can get you a ton of clicks, but like most everything else when it comes to mortgage lead generation—without proper landing pages, you'll get little or nothing out of it.

Also, mobile traffic on Facebook is huge, with over 50% of users only logging in from mobile devices, so using landing pages that are optimized for mobile will be critical for success.

There's a lot you need to get familiar with to make Facebook ads work for you—using Facebook's ad manager or power editor, selecting the right ad type depending on your objective, crafting effective headlines, creating banners, targeting the right audience, and more.

I'm going to cover these things in the following sections, and the beauty of it is that just about anyone can get the hang of it, allowing you to quickly tap into a lot of business and opportunities that your competitors are missing out on.

Once you're familiar with the basics, you can, of course, have an assistant, virtual assistant, or marketing manager run ads for you.

It's still important, however, to have an understanding of what works and what doesn't, and be able to give the person running ads for you some direction on what kinds of ads you want them to focus on.

I go into a fair amount of detail in the next sections of this chapter, but know that it's not meant to serve as a complete front-to-back guide on Facebook ad creation and strategy.

This is just a high-level overview that will give you a head start and point you in the right direction.

As mentioned before, Facebook is changing things and adding new options regularly, but the main points I emphasize in the following sections of this chapter should still be relevant (unless there's a complete overhaul of Facebook's ad dashboard that makes these concepts obsolete).

In that case, or in the event of any large or meaningful update to Facebook's ad dashboard, this book will be updated to reflect those changes.

Regardless, the main thing is to always test new ads and campaigns.

What's working now may not work in a few months, and offers that work in one city or state may not work well in others. The same is true with times and days of the week you post, images you use, language in your headlines, and just about everything else... Keep on testing.

It's not expensive, you can get feedback quickly, and the upside of learning new strategies and uncovering hidden gems makes the cost of trying new things with your Facebook ad campaigns well worth it.

Setting Up Your Ads

Once again: Facebook's ad creation interface is constantly being updated, and this book will be updated regularly to reflect any changes that are worth noting.

For updates to this book and more, go to:

www.leadPops.com/manifesto-updates

When logged into Facebook, use the arrow menu on the top right to select "Create Ads".

Figure 8-1: this drop down menu is accessible from the top right corner of Facebook's main navigation bar.

Once you click "Create Ads", you can use the hamburger menu at the top left of the next screen to select between "Ads Manager" or "Power Editor", as shown in Figure 8-2.

Figure 8-2: this drop down menu is accessible from the top left corner of Facebook's ad creation dashboard, allowing you to select between the Ads Manager and the Power Editor.

Facebook lets you choose between two different tools for creating ads:

▶ **Ad Manager**

https://www.facebook.com/ads/manager/creation

▶ **Power Editor**

https://www.facebook.com/ads/manage/powereditor

Though the Ads Manager is great for dipping your toe in the water, it doesn't offer as much flexibility for ad creation, so I'm going to explain the basics of Power Editor in the following segments.

Select "Power Editor".
Next, click "Create Campaign".
That will take you through the steps below.

At the time of this writing (August 2016), ads can be broken down into three main sections:

1. Campaign—objective

2. Ad Set—conversions, audience, placements, budget, and schedule

3. Ads—media and text

Creating an "Ideal Customer Persona"

We're going to go through each of these in detail, but before doing that, it's important for you to understand a very elementary principal for marketing—knowing your ideal customer persona.

Who is it you're going after? What are their goals, values, possible objections, demographics, age, sex, location, wants, desires, struggles, sources of information, etc.?

You want to identify these things in as much details as possible before you start putting together your ads, and each ad/campaign should have its own customer persona to go with it.

The more accurate this is, the better you'll relate to your customers and the more effective your ads and offers will be.

To help out, I've created a simple "Ideal Customer Persona" workbook you can download for free. Just to go:

www.leadPops.com/manifesto-bonus

Step 1: Campaign

Objective

The first thing you'll need to do is select your campaign "objective" from the following options:

- ► Boost Your Posts
- ► Promote Your Page
- ► Send People to Your Website
- ► Increase Conversions on Your Website
- ► Get Installs on Your App
- ► Increase Engagement in Your App
- ► Reach People Near Your Business
- ► Raise Attendance at Your Event
- ► Get People to Claim your Offer

- ► Get Video Views
- ► Promote a Product Catalog
- ► Collect Leads for Your Business
- ► Increase Brand Awareness

Assuming you've got some good landing pages to work with, we're going to start with the objective, "Increase Conversions on Your Website".

"Send People to Your Website" is <u>almost</u> the same thing, but doesn't require a tracking pixel to be placed on your landing page, which means conversion tracking would be manual and not available in Facebook's reporting.

A tracking pixel isn't a requirement, but if you've got the technical knowledge, or can get help adding it (literally copying and pasting the pixel code into the code of the landing page), then I recommend it.

If not, go ahead with the "Send People to Your Website" option so you can get started and get some experience.

Another ad objective that's worth testing is: "Collect Leads for Your Business", where you can actually build custom lead capture forms directly into Facebook, along with auto-fill functionality for users' contact information. Check that out and test it once you have some experience with the more basic click-through ads.

Step 2: Ad Set

Conversions

Your objective is to "increase conversions", so to track that, Facebook will provide you with a tracking pixel.

First, they'll need you to select a conversion goal.

In this case, select "Lead", as shown in Figure 8-3.

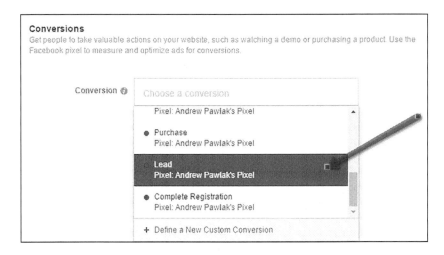

Figure 8-3: this drop down menu is at the top of the Power Editor dashboard when "Increase Conversions on Your Website" is your objective.

Next, a window will pop up with the pixel code and instructions to copy and paste it between the <head> and </head> in your landing page code. The pixel will track visits to your landing page and conversions.

You can also email this code directly to whoever handles your web stuff for you, like an assistant, marketing manager, or your web guy/gal, and have them place the tracking pixel for you.

(At leadPops, we install tracking pixels on landing pages and websites for clients every day. It's easy and takes no more than a minute to setup.)

Audience (Targeting)

The level of targeting you're able to achieve with Facebook is unparalleled. This is where it gets fun.

"**Custom Audiences**" gives you the option to upload targeted lists using email addresses, phone numbers, Facebook user IDs or app user IDs, to create and save audiences you'd like to show ads to.

You can also create a "**New Custom Audience**", which allows you to reach people who have a relationship with your business, whether they are existing customers or people who have interacted with your business on Facebook or other platforms.

These options include:

- ► **Customer File:** use a customer file (CSV or TXT) to match your customers with people on Facebook and create an audience from the matches. The data will be hashed prior to upload.

- ► **Website Traffic:** create a list of people who visit your website or view specific web pages.

- ► **App Activity:** create a list of people who have taken a specific action in your app or game.

- ► **Engagement on Facebook:** create a list of people who have engaged with your content on Facebook.

"**Location**" lets you target potential clients by state(s), market(s), specific city (or cities), or within a 10-50 mile radius of any geographic location, including or excluding specific areas you do or don't want to advertise in.

Location also lets you drill down by:
- ► Everyone in this Location
- ► People Who Live in this Location
- ► People recently in this Location
- ► People Traveling to this Location

Additional targeting options include:

- ▶ Age range
- ▶ Gender
- ▶ Language

Then you have "**Detailed Targeting**", which includes:

Demographics—

- ▶ Education
- ▶ Ethnic Affinity
- ▶ Financial
- ▶ Generation
- ▶ Home
- ▶ Life Events
- ▶ Parents
- ▶ Politics (US)
- ▶ Relationship
- ▶ Work

Interests—

- ▶ Business & Industry
- ▶ Entertainment
- ▶ Family & Relationships
- ▶ Fitness & Wellness
- ▶ Food & Drink
- ▶ Hobbies & Activities
- ▶ Shopping & Fashion
- ▶ Sports & Outdoors
- ▶ Technology

Behaviors—

- ▶ Automotive
- ▶ B2B
- ▶ Charitable Donations

- ► Consumer Classification
- ► Digital Activities
- ► Expats
- ► Financial
- ► Job Role
- ► Media
- ► Mobile Device User
- ► Purchase Behavior
- ► Residential Profiles
- ► Seasonal & Events
- ► Travel

There are multiple sublevels for each of these categories, allowing you to build custom audiences that include (or exclude) people that fall into any of them.

This means you can cast an insanely wide net, or get incredibly granular with your targeting.

For example, you can create and target an audience that includes only:

English-speaking women living within a 30 mile radius of any city you want to target... who are "stay-at-home" moms between the ages of 25-45... that are married, currently renting, and health nuts... And are potential first time homebuyers... and drive a car that's paid off worth $50,000 or more... and earn between $100,000-$350,000 per year.

And excludes: recent homebuyers and recent mortgage borrowers...

And that's not even scratching the surface...

Figure 8-4 shows a snapshot of what that audience looks like inside the Power Editor dashboard:

Audience Definition

Your audience is defined.

Specific — Broad

Audience Details:

- Location - Living In:
  - United States: San Diego (+30 mi) California
- Age:
  - 25 - 45
- Gender:
  - Female
- Placements:
  - on pages: News Feed on desktop computers, News Feed on mobile devices, Right column on desktop computers, Third-party Apps and Websites on mobile devices or Instagram Feed
- Exclude:
  - Behaviors: Recent homebuyer or Recent mortgage borrower
- People Who Match:
  - Behaviors: $50,000 - $75,000 or Over $75,000
  - Relationship Status: Married
  - Income: $100,000 - $125,000, $125,000 - $150,000, $150,000 - $250,000 or $250,000 - $350,000
  - Home Ownership: First time homebuyer or Renters
  - Moms: Stay-at-home moms

Potential Reach: 260,000 people

Estimated Daily Reach

560 - 1,500 people on Facebook

0   of 200,000

540 - 1,400 people on Instagram

0   of 80,000

This is only an estimate. Numbers shown are based on the average performance of ads targeted to your selected audience.

Figure 8-4: Facebook provides you with a summary of your target audience with information like "Potential Reach" which is the total estimated reach based on your targeting settings, and "Estimated Daily Reach", which is based on your budget/ad spend.

As you can imagine, you've got to be strategic when setting up your audiences.

You can go after active military, veterans, doctors, lawyers, company vice presidents, people with a net worth of over $1M, people with their Master's degrees, college grads, golfers, investors, individuals with premium credit cards, those that travel frequently, and much more.

Or, conversely, you can target everybody between the ages of 22-65 that lives in your state...

Your audience selection depends on your ideal customer persona and offer.

Don't forget: it pays to test different targeting strategies.

B2B allows you to go after other business professionals.

Here's another concept: create ads targeting Realtors® with messaging that talks about your successful marketing programs. Explain that you share qualified buyer and seller leads with your partner agents—unlike other LOs who typically don't bring any business to the table and just expect referrals.

These ads would, of course, point to a landing page where you could include a quick intro video, outline your USP (Unique Selling Proposition), and include some of the ways you provide agents with leads, along with a smart form that qualifies agents that are interested to see if they're eligible for your program...

Base eligibility on average # of transactions they close per year, their marketing, and other qualifying factors—those are the kinds of questions you'd ask on your "Agent Qualifier" form to make sure they're a good fit.

More strategy on building better Realtor® relationships in Chapter 12.

"**Connections**" enables you to reach people who have a specific kind of connection to your Facebook page, app, or event.

This will narrow your audience to include only people with that specific connection who also meet the other targeting categories you've selected.

Connection types include:

▶ **Facebook Pages**

- People who like your page
- Friends of people who like your page
- Exclude people who like your page

▶ **Apps**

- People who used your app
- Friends of people who used your app
- Exclude people who used your app

▶ **Events**

- People who responded to your event
- Friends of people who responded to your event
- Exclude people who responded to your event

There are countless strategies to consider, and it's certainly fun to brainstorm the various ways you can make money with Facebook ads as a mortgage professional...

But the most important thing is that you jump in there and get started!

Get some experience.

Don't over think it.

Setup some basic targeting to start out and once you begin getting some data from the ads you're running, you can fine-tune your campaigns and experiment with new ideas.

As always, testing is the key to determining what works well in your market.

Once you create and save an audience that works, you can choose Facebook's "Lookalike Audience" feature, which allows you to reach people on Facebook who are similar to your select audiences.

And keep in mind: as a mortgage professional, you earn a pretty good chunk of money when you make a sale.

That means you have plenty of wiggle room to figure things out with Facebook ads before you're in the red and out of the realm where 1 deal pays for your learning curve.

So don't give up if you've spent a couple hundred bucks and haven't closed a deal. Stick with it and you're likely to strike gold, repeatedly, once you get the swing of it.

Placements

You can choose where you want your ads to show on Facebook. Placement options include:

- ► Mobile News Feed
- ► Instagram
- ► Audience Network (Facebook approved partner mobile apps and websites)
- ► Desktop Newsfeed
- ► Desktop Right Column

Decide whether you want automatic placement across places most likely to reach the right people, which Facebook recommends, or if you want to manually include or exclude any of the placements listed above.

For example: Facebook on mobile pulls a <u>ton</u> of traffic, but if you don't have a great mobile landing page, then you need to exclude mobile traffic until you have a solid mobile landing page destination ready.

Also, I recommend turning "Audience Network" OFF for cold traffic.

Test, test, test!

Budget and Schedule

Facebook's interface lets you easily setup your budget with options for:

- **Daily Budget:** I recommend no less than $10/day. A daily budget lets you run your ad continuously starting the day you launch, or setup a start and end date.

- **Lifetime Budget:** once again, I recommend a minimum of $10/day ($300-$400/month), which has a start and end date along with whatever budget you allocate for that time period.

Facebook lets you turn ads on/off whenever you want, no matter what budget type you pick.

"**Optimization for Ad Delivery**" lets you choose how you want Facebook to deliver ads to people based on the "objective" you're trying to achieve.

You've already determined the objective at the beginning, in this case— "Increase Conversions on Your Website"—so keep the "Optimization for Ad Delivery" option on "Conversions", which you'll see is recommended based on that objective (you can test other options later, if you want).

"**Conversion Window**" is the length of time between someone clicking or viewing your ad and completing a valuable action you've defined as a conversion event.

The window you choose here lets Facebook know whether to focus on 1 day or 7 days' worth of conversion data when determining who should see your ad.

To start out, keep this option on "1 Day Window"—you can always adjust this later.

"**Bid Amount**" gives you options for "automatic" and "manual"— keep this on automatic for now, test later if you'd like (once you have more experience).

"**When You Get Charged**" determines when you pay for your ad.

For many optimization goals, you'll pay each time your ad is served (known as an impression).

Some optimization goals also let you choose between impressions and actions (such as link clicks or post engagements).

For the objective of increasing conversions on your website, your selection here will automatically be set to CPM (cost per thousand impressions; M = Roman numeral for 1K) and not customizable.

"**Ad Scheduling**" will let you set it up to either run ads all the time, or on a customized schedule. Scheduling only works with a "Lifetime Budget".

Don't start out with scheduling unless you already have experience and know what works in your market.

First you need some data that tells you what's pulling best before you start making decisions as to what days and times you want to show ads.

Once you have some information to work with, you can test different times and days, weekends, etc. and focus your efforts on what's working best for you.

"**Delivery Type**" offers the following options:

▶ **Standard:** show your ads throughout the day—recommended and the preferred option for most advertisers.

▶ **Accelerated:** show your ads as quickly as possible—can be useful for promoting time-sensitive events and quickly reaching a target audience.

"**Ad Set Name**" is the name you choose and should be something you can easily identify the ad set with.

Step 3: Ads

Here's where we get into creating the actual ads. As of August 2016, Facebook ads for driving people to your website or landing page are made up of the following components:

▶ **Ad Name:** only seen by you/your Facebook admins.

▶ **Select Facebook Page:** which of your Facebook pages you want this ad to show it's coming from.

▶ **Select Ad with 1 Image or Video OR Ad with Multiple Images or Videos in a Carousel:** to start out, use 1 image; test the other options once you've gotten some experience.

▶ **Image or Video:** determine what kind of ad you want to create and select which one you want to use.

▶ **Upload Image or Video:** upload a file from your computer or a previous file you've uploaded to Facebook.

- ▶ **Website URL or Canvas:** where people will be taken when they click on your ad; "Canvas" is a much more advanced option and something you can test down the road.

- ▶ **Display URL:** the link as you want people to see it in your ad.

- ▶ **Text:** the text that tells people about what you're promoting.

- ▶ **Headline:** brief headliner describing where people will visit—your headline text will appear differently depending on the placement of your ad; check the previews to make sure your headline looks the way you want in the placements it appears in.

- ▶ **News Feed Link Description:** describe your link and why people should click it.

- ▶ **Call-to-action:** choose the action you want people to take when they see your ad; this will show as a button with whatever text you select from the options in the "Call-to-Action" drop down menu.

Figure 8-5: these are the main visual components of Facebook ads. The image area can be multiple images displayed in a carousel, or a video.

Facebook has a "Preview" area on the right side of the screen that shows you what your ad looks like as you assemble it.

This preview area also has options that let you toggle between the different placements you've selected so you can know what your ad will look like across the various areas it will be seen—desktop, desktop right column, mobile, etc.

Next, I'm going to show you a few different examples of ads for real estate and mortgage with the objective of increasing conversions on your landing page or website, or, if you're not using the tracking pixel, sending people to your landing page (or website).

Facebook Ad Examples

Ad Example 1: Real Estate Property Listings

You can get your hands on listings to market from Realtors® you're working with.

Let them know you've got a lead generation strategy that will help them get more serious buyers with some unique and untapped ways to market their properties. Once you get the OK, you're ready to go.

All the information you need regarding properties you're interested in using to generate leads can be found on an agent's website, the MLS, or a real estate portal, like Realtor.com.

Grabbing the information is as simple as copying and pasting details from a website into Facebook's dashboard, and right-clicking to save images in a folder on your desktop and then uploading those images to Facebook (like adding an attachment to an email).

Once you get the hang of it, I recommend hiring an offshore virtual assistant to prepare ads like the ones shown below for you for around $5/hour. That way you can focus on selling and building relationships, not playing marketing guy/gal.

I provide a couple great resources for hiring virtual assistants in Chapter 34.

Keep in mind: you're going to be generating leads for yourself and for your agents, while building better, more loyal Realtor® partnerships. It's a win-win for everyone.

I'm going to provide a lot of detail on tactics pertaining to this first ad example, most of which you'll be able to apply to the rest of the example ads that follow.

Here's an example of a property listing ad:

Desktop News Feed View:

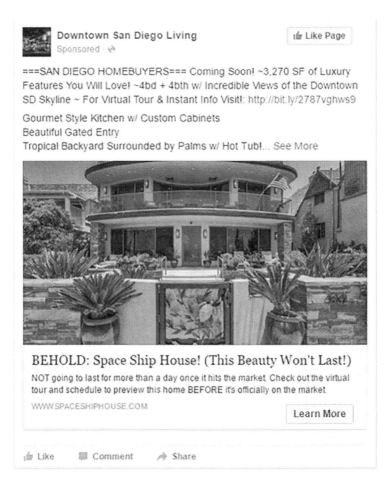

Figure 8-6: this preview of the ad shows you how it will look in the desktop news feed.

Mobile News Feed View:

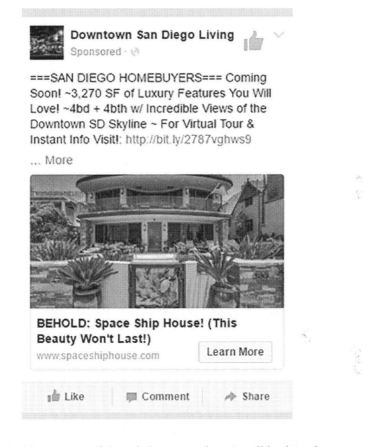

Figure 8-7: this preview of the ad shows you how it will look in the mobile news feed.

Desktop Right Column View:

BEHOLD: Space Ship House! (This Beauty...
www.spaceshiphouse.com
===SAN DIEGO HOMEBUYERS=== Coming
Soon! 3,270 SF of Luxury Features You Will
Love! ~4bd +...

Figure 8-8: this preview of the ad shows you how it will look in the desktop right column.

Key Ad Components Include:

1. Local community page: "Downtown San Diego Living".

2. "San Diego Homebuyers" text calls out to specific audience based on targeting and audience selection settings.

3. "Coming Soon" text conveys exclusivity/scarcity.

4. Property description doesn't include pricing, which means people who are interested have to click into the ad to get that crucial information; it does include, however, amenities and features that make the listing unique and attractive.

5. URL shortened using www.Bitly.com (free tool)—use this tool if the page you're driving visitors to has a long and ugly URL scheme.

6. The clickable URL in the text shows before Facebook truncates the rest of the copy with "See More" on desktop and mobile news feed placements.

7. Headline stands out with the text, "BEHOLD: Space Ship House!" and includes, "This Beauty Won't Last!", which helps create a sense of urgency.

8. Also, I recommend testing curiosity-based messaging, like "Must See Inside!" or "You WON'T Believe the Master Bedroom!"

9. "Learn More" CTA button shows on both desktop and mobile newsfeed placements. I recommend testing different CTA buttons for various ads to see what draws in the most clicks. You can also select "no button" and see how that works for you.

10. Ad clicks take users to a conversion optimized "**single property page**" with more detailed information, pictures, video (if available), and several related lead conversion points, including:
    * Schedule Showing
    * Request Information
    * Get Pre-Approved
    * Search More Homes
    * Find Home Values

Conversion-Optimized Single Property Pages:

If your single property pages are not optimized for lead conversion, what good are they?

Here's how a conversion-optimized property landing page should look and function:

Figure 8-9: this single property page is optimized to convert leads with the following options to capture buyer contact information: "Schedule Showing" and "Request Property Report" + additional built-in lead generation landing pages for "Get-Pre-Approved", "Search More Homes", and "Find Home Values".

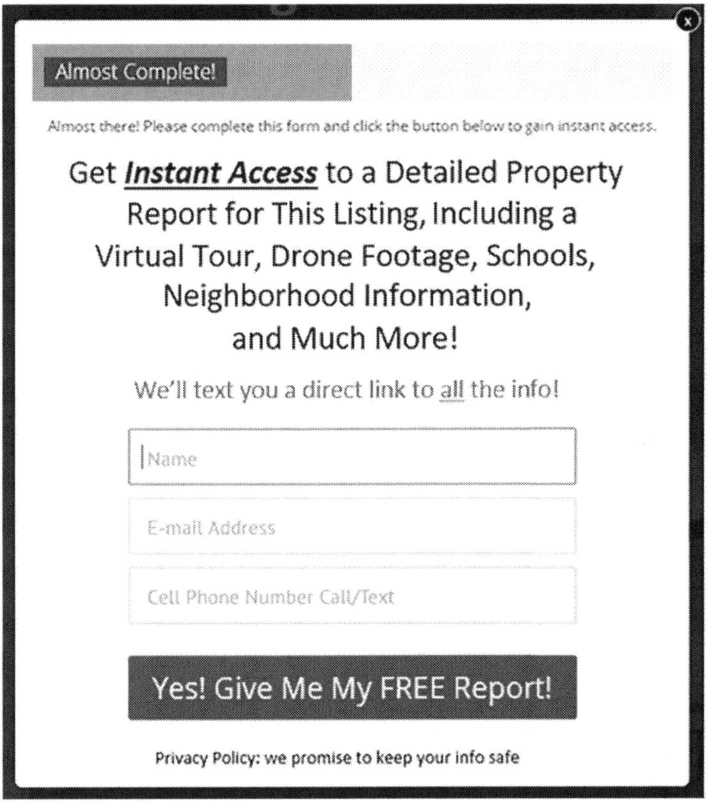

Figure 8-10: this click-triggered popup is an example of the kind of lead capture form that opens up on top of the listing when the viewer clicks "Request Property Report" or "Schedule Showing".

Real Estate Landing Pages:

The anatomy of a high-converting real estate landing page is very similar to that of a mortgage landing page described in Chapter 2.

The main differences are the messaging and form questions, which need to match the CTA, whether it's an offer to search homes, find home values, or whatever it is you're promoting.

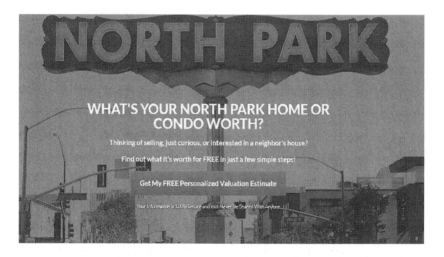

Figure 8-11: a click-through landing page for home values with an orange CTA button above the fold that takes the user to a gamified multi-step lead generation form.

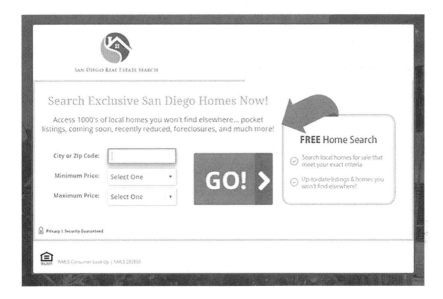

Figure 8-12: a lead generation landing page for real estate searches. The gamified multi-step lead generation form captures the buyers' search criteria and contact information before taking them to a customized display of properties (MLS listings, or a Realtor's® property search results page on their website, which creates a fantastic partnership opportunity).

Ad Example 2: Real Estate Searches

For this ad concept, you can upload a photo of a local listing, or use Facebook's "stock photo" option, which comes up when you click to upload an image in the ad creation area of Facebook's dashboard.

Be sure to select a photo that matches the search you're promising in your offer.

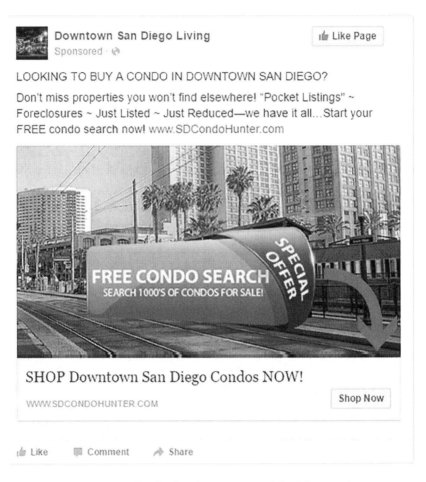

Figure 8-13: an example of a "real estate search" ad for condos in Downtown San Diego. This is the "desktop news feed" view.

Key Ad Components Include:

1. Local community page: "Downtown San Diego Living".

2. "LOOKING TO BUY A CONDO IN DOWNTOWN SAN DIEGO?" calls out to a specific audience based on targeting and audience selection settings.

3. Ad text conveys exclusivity/scarcity—"don't miss properties you won't find elsewhere" and "'Pocket Listings' ~ Foreclosures ~ Just Listed ~ Just Reduced— we have it all..." + sense of urgency CTA text—"Start your FREE condo search now!".

4. Additional "button" graphic overlay on top of a relevant image for "Downtown San Diego", with an arrow pointing to Facebook's built-in call-to-action button option for "Shop Now". Remember: you have access to 700+ CTA buttons for free at: www.leadPops.com/manifesto-bonus

5. The button graphic overlay and arrow were added to the image using an awesome website called: www.Canva.com (no affiliation to leadPops).

6. Display URL matches the messaging (make sure whatever display URL you use is actually a domain you own or you may end up driving traffic to somebody else's website).

7. Ad takes people that click to a "condo search" lead generation landing page that collects search criteria and contact info, then sends them to relevant properties (or provides a thank you page letting them know you'll follow-up with an exclusive listings report that features properties that match their criteria).

8. Headline stands out with the text "SHOP Downtown San Diego Condos NOW!" and helps create a sense of urgency.

Ad Example 3: Exclusive Property Reports ("Just Reduced")

This kind of ad can be used for "Just Reduced" properties, and other exclusive listings like: foreclosures, short sales, list of homes that qualify for zero down, 203K, USDA, and much more.

As always, make sure you've setup strategic targeting, the ad copy matches the landing page, and after collecting information, you either take the user directly to listings that match their search criteria, or let them know on your thank you page (with either text or a video) that you will be following up with an exclusive report that includes properties that meet their search criteria ASAP.

From there, you simply hand that lead off to a Realtor® partner and have them prepare the list of properties for the prospect.

Your job on these leads, of course, is to get the buyers pre-approved, so use the follow-up as an opportunity to build rapport and explain all the benefits of getting pre-approved as soon as possible.

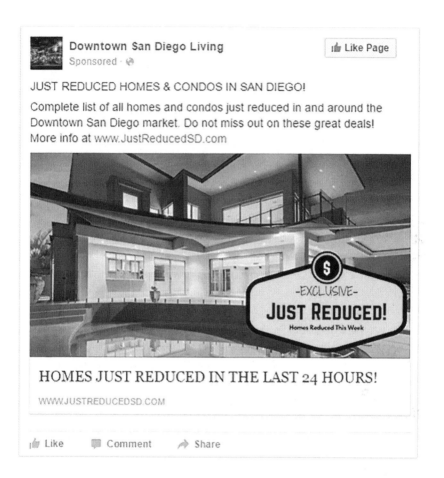

Figure 8-14: an example of an "Exclusive Property Reports" ad for "Just Reduced" homes and condos in San Diego. This is the "desktop news feed" view.

Key Ad Components Include:

1. Local community page: "Downtown San Diego Living".

2. "JUST REDUCED HOMES & CONDOS IN SAN DIEGO!" calls out to a specific audience based on targeting and audience selection settings.

3. Ad text conveys exclusivity/scarcity—"complete list of homes and condos just reduced..." and "don't miss out on these great deals!"

4. Additional text/graphic overlay added to image using www.Canva.com (no affiliation to leadPops).

5. Ad takes user to a "home finder" lead generation landing page that collects home criteria and contact info, then sends them to relevant properties (or provides a thank you page letting them know you'll follow-up with an exclusive listings report that features properties that match their criteria).

6. Headline stands out with the text "HOMES JUST REDUCED IN THE LAST 24 HOURS!" and helps create a sense of urgency.

Ad Example #4: 203K Loans/Listings

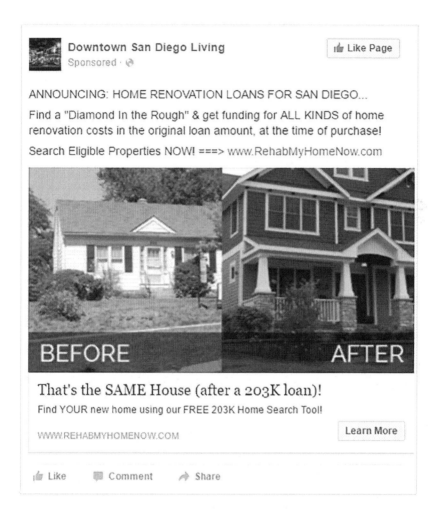

Figure 8-15: an example of another "Exclusive Property Reports" ad for "203K Eligible Properties" in San Diego. This is the "desktop news feed" view.

Ad Example #5: Down Payment Assistance

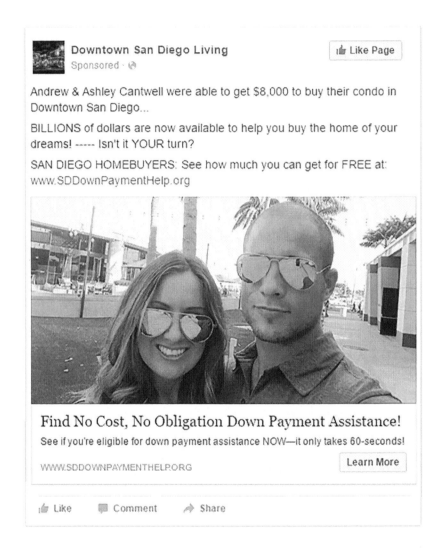

Figure 8-16: an example of a "Down Payment Assistance" ad. This is the "desktop news feed" view.

Ad Example #6: Home Values Offer

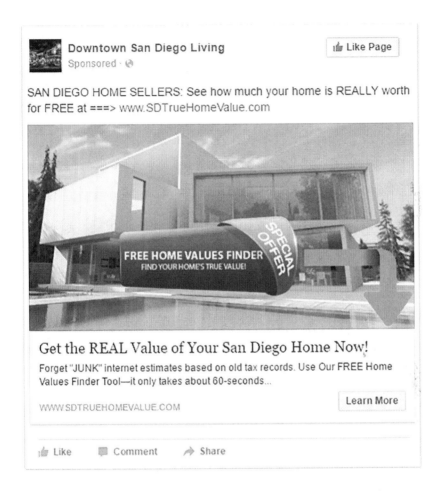

Figure 8-17: an example of a "Home Values" ad. This is the "desktop news feed" view.

Ad Example #7: Pre-Approval Offer (a)

Figure 8-18: an example of a "Pre-Approval" ad. This is the "desktop news feed" view.

Pre-Approval Offer (b)

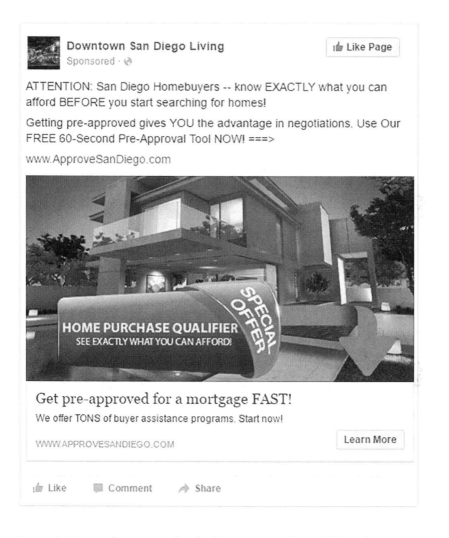

Figure 8-19: another example of a "Pre-Approval" ad. This is the "desktop news feed" view.

Ad Example #8: Refinance Analysis Offer (a)

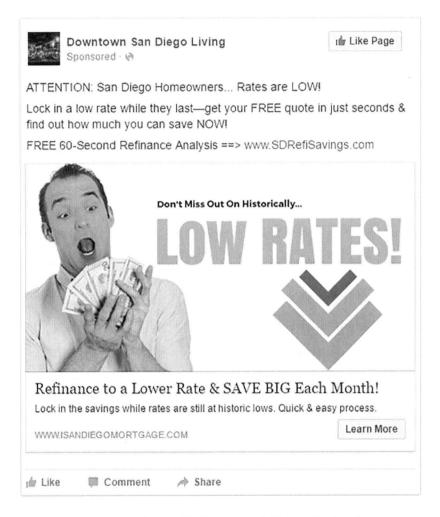

Figure 8-20: an example of a "Refinance" ad. This is the "desktop news feed" view.

Refinance Analysis Offer (b)

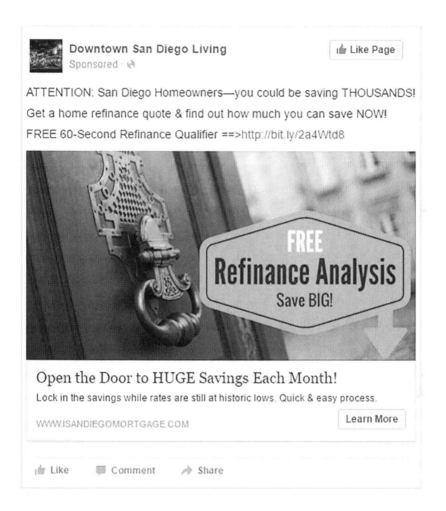

Figure 8-21: another example of a "Refinance" ad. This is the "desktop news feed" view.

Ad Example #9: Rent vs. Buy

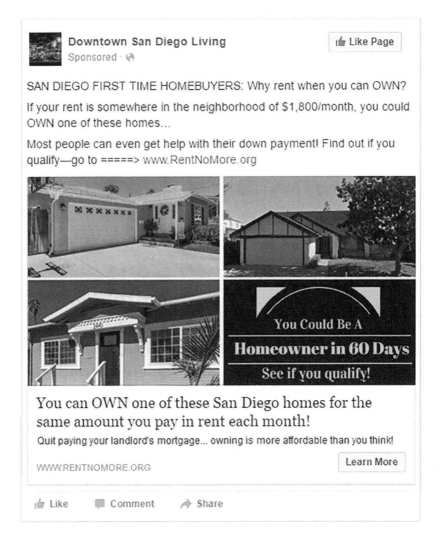

Figure 8-22: an example of a "Rent vs. Buy" ad. This is the "desktop news feed" view.

Ad Example #10: USDA Loans/Listings

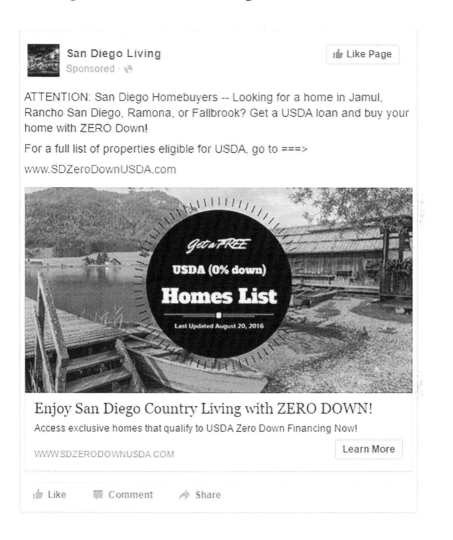

Figure 8-23: an example of an "Exclusive Properties Report" ad for "USDA Eligible Properties" in San Diego. This is the "desktop news feed" view.

Ad Example #11: VA Loans

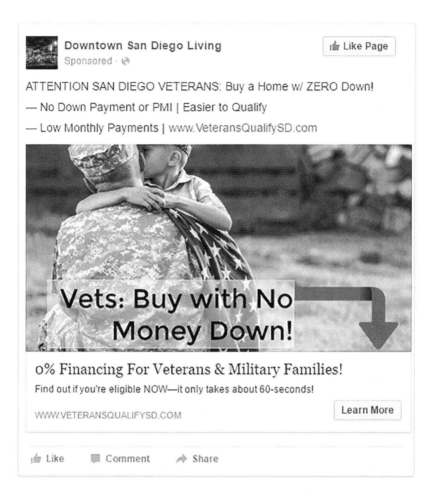

Figure 8-24: an example of a "VA Loans" ad. This is the "desktop news feed" view.

Ad Example #12: Zero Down Loans/Listings

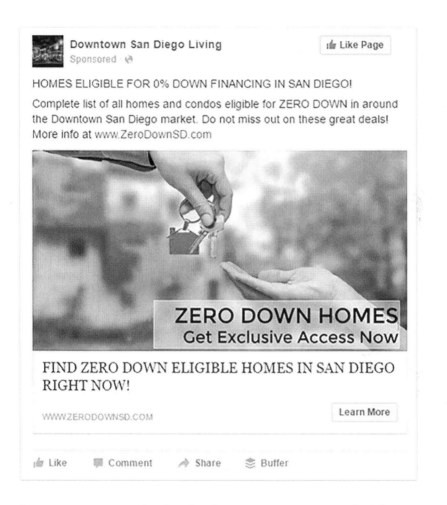

Figure 8-25: an example of an "Exclusive Properties Report" ad for "Zero Down Eligible Properties" in San Diego. This is the "desktop news feed" view.

Facebook Ads Reporting

Facebook provides in-depth reporting on ad campaigns, offering everything you need to know about the performance of your ads.

This includes: total spend, number of clicks/impressions, cost per click/impression, breakdowns of top performing placements and devices, and much more.

For detailed information on Facebook ad reporting (and all kinds of other tutorials regarding Facebook ads), go to:

www.facebook.com/business (search "reporting")

Facebook Ads Summary

You can generate a ton of leads with a good Facebook advertising strategy.

The keys to success are: setting up the right targeting along with strong, matching offers based on your objective, and using conversion-optimized landing pages to convert clicks into qualified leads.

Make sure you test everything on an ongoing basis.

Also, be sure to create new ads often and rotate them frequently. "Ad fatigue" (resulting in a drop in click-through rates) happens if you fail to change them up regularly. Your audience becomes accustomed to your ads and tunes them out.

CHAPTER 9

Launch a Retargeting Campaign

Retargeting automatically keeps track of the people who visit your website, landing pages, blog, etc. by planting a pixel in their browser, which allows you to begin "following" them with display ads (banners) as they visit other sites online—Facebook, ESPN, MSN, Yahoo, YouTube, and thousands of the most popular sites on the web.

The pixel is not noticeable. In fact, you've probably been retargeted countless times online without even knowing it.

Ever viewed something on Amazon without purchasing, then every other website you go to shows an ad for that item? That's retargeting.

You can also retarget custom audiences based on an email list, allowing you to stay in front of your past clients, referral partners, and even leads that didn't close.

You'll get the best results from retargeting if you segment your visitors (i.e.—people who looked at a refinance page vs. those looking to buy a home) and tailor the retargeting ads shown to each group.

Or, you can choose to not retarget them at all (i.e.—people who've already converted).

Here are some of the top retargeting platforms (no affiliation to leadPops):

► www.Adroll.com

► www.PerfectAudience.com

► www.SiteScout.com

Retargeting is relatively inexpensive, it's effective, and it works for you 24/7.

If you're spending money on marketing and driving traffic, retargeting is definitely something you should be taking advantage of to help you get the most bang for your buck.

Bonus: For an in depth guide on retargeting visit:

www.leadPops.com/manifesto-bonus

CHAPTER 10
Email Signature CRO

Your email signature gives you a prime opportunity to optimize for lead conversion.

Simply adding a link with a strong call-to-action that takes email recipients to a landing page can help bring in additional leads and loans.

Keep in mind: "Apply Now" with a link to a 1003 application is <u>not</u> a good call-to-action or lead generation strategy.

Your emails are getting viewed by thousands of people per year, and often times forwarded between Realtors®, borrowers and their family members, appraisers, title reps, escrow agents, and other professionals involved in the transaction.

Use your email signature as a tool to grow your leads and referrals, not just a listing for your phone number and business address.

Another idea is to include something like:

"Realtors®: learn how I can help YOU generate more qualified leads and sell more homes—<u>Click Here</u>!"

That would take any interested agent to a landing page that you have set up that talks about your marketing and lead generation programs, inviting them to apply if they qualify.

Optimizing your email signature is a simple, one-time fix. It only takes a few minutes to setup, it's free, and it can help you pull in some extra loans.

And remember: it's all about branding YOU.

Figure 10-1: an example of a branded email signature optimized with a CTA button that points to a "free rate quote" lead generation landing page.

CHAPTER 11

Voicemail Message CRO

Your voicemail message gives you another opportunity to convert leads.

Simply referencing an easy domain name with a strong call-to-action that takes callers to a website or landing page designed for lead conversion can bring in additional business.

Once again, telling people to "Apply Online" and directing them to a loan application is not a good call-to-action or lead generation strategy.

Instead of the generic, "I'm not here right now. Please leave a message and I'll call you back," give people immediate service and provide direction to move things forward.

You don't want to leave potential clients sitting around and waiting for a call back (that's IF they even leave a message and let you know how to get back to them), or worse, hanging up and calling another LO.

People want immediate gratification. They have countless options when shopping for a mortgage, so if they don't get a hold of you, they're likely to move on to the next person on their list, or business card they have from an agent that gave them 2 or 3 referrals.

Use this script to change your voicemail and get more potential clients in contact with you when you can't help with them right then and there:

"Hello and thank for calling _____."

"At the moment, I'm helping another client with a home purchase or refinance, but for IMMEDIATE service, go to—"

"(WWW.YOUR-DOMAIN-NAME.COM)"

"There, you can get a HASSLE-FREE, customized rate quote... fast & easy, 24/7!"

"It only takes about 60 seconds to submit the information online and I'll follow-up promptly to let you know exactly what I can do for you."

"Again, that web address is—."

"(WWW.YOUR-DOMAIN-NAME.COM)"

"For any other questions, please leave a message and I'll will get back to you as soon as I can."

"Thanks and I look forward to speaking with you soon."

Again, the domain name referenced should take users to a landing page or website that's optimized for lead conversion, otherwise it doesn't do you or the potential client any good.

The goal is to use your voicemail as a tool to grow your leads and referrals by offering an option for immediate service, not just a message promising to call people back.

Like your email signature, optimizing your voicemail is a simple, one-time fix that only takes a few minutes to setup, it's free, and it works.

CHAPTER 12

Establish Better Realtor® Relationships & Recruit 3-5+ New Realtor® Partners

A lot of the mortgage professionals I've worked with over the years have told me that real estate agents are difficult to work with. Many would say that's a nice way of putting it.

Although not in the same capacity, I've worked with Realtors® for the last 12 years.

As a whole, they're no more difficult to work with than mortgage professionals, insurance agents, or any other type of business professional/small business owner.

Some of them are awesome, some are a pain in the butt. You've got folks on both ends of the spectrum and everywhere in between.

That's how it is with everything.

The fact is: as a mortgage originator, if you play your cards right and learn how to play the game, Realtors® can make you a LOT of money.

You also need to be empathetic and understand that Realtors® are getting hit up by mortgage people for referrals every single day.

Nonstop.

Agents might as well keep a fishbowl on their desk for LO business cards and setup a separate vm box for all the loan officers hitting them up trying to get their foot in the door for referrals.

That's where a lot of the loyalty issues come in.

You've got real estate agent/loan officer relationships, which, most of the time, are a one-way street when it comes to referrals.

On top of that, these agents are getting bombarded all the time by new loan officers trying to outdo each other—offering all kinds of goodies, from dinners to ballgame tickets, paying for marketing with MSAs, etc.

Everybody says they'll do a good job on the loan, they'll close on time, they've got great communication... Yada, yada, yada.

So, what separates you from the other 25 loan officers that are approaching the same Realtors® you're talking to, also asking for business?

How are you going to prevent the next LO that comes along with a decent value offering from snagging one of your producing agents out from under you?

Here's the key that's going to separate you from all that noise:

Bringing REAL VALUE to the table.

Not donuts or rate sheets, or promises of impeccable customer service.

And you definitely don't want to just start paying for half of their marketing with your fingers crossed hoping that they'll eventually refer you a deal.

That hardly ever works, and when it does, it's not the position you want to be in.

You don't want to be chasing real estate agents around with your hand out because you paid for something.

A good place to start is by gaining understanding of what the obstacles are in building new Realtor® relationships. Once you do, they're a lot easier to overcome.

For example: any Realtor® that's worth talking to already has loan officers they're comfortable working with.

Pretty obvious, right?

You need to disrupt their existing loan officer relationships; you have to get the in-house mortgage person out of the equation, and establish loyalty.

And all of that is a lot easier than you might think.

The fact is, Realtor® co-marketing is broken.

You could spend a life-time chasing around the wrong agents with a revolving door of Realtors® that seem hot one minute and then never return your calls the next.

You don't want that.

Neither do I—that's why I wrote this chapter.

The strategy I'm going to share with you does not entail you becoming their marketing assistant, or some lengthy honeymooning process.

What I'm going to show you is how to:

1. **Find the RIGHT Realtors®.**

   We call these your "WHALE Agents" WHALE stands for Worth Helping A Little Extra. These are producers that you enjoy (or at least can tolerate) working with that are in a position to refer you at least 1 client/deal every 30-60 days. Not 1 referral—1 sale.

2. **Approach the relationship from a position of strength.**

   You don't want to find yourself genuflecting to real estate agents and groveling for their referrals.

That's not going to be needed when you're actually bringing them business (while generating your own exclusive leads).

That's what this strategy is all about.

Just like you can't sell a mortgage to a click, Realtors® can't sell houses to clicks.

Chances are, if they're doing any marketing (SPOILER ALERT—those are the ones you want get in with!) — they're getting a lot of traffic with very few leads...

Or, just as bad, they get a ton of leads, and almost none of them close. They have a quality issue.

A lot of times, it's both—they don't get enough leads and the leads they get don't close at a high rate.

Those are two key and universal pain points for Realtors®.

This strategy lets YOU step in and bring a solution.

That's going to be your USP. And it's one you can take to the bank... literally.

Realtors® want to close more deals, and you can make that happen.

Good WHALE Hunting: Strategy for Establishing NEW Realtor® Partners

First, start by making a list of the real estate agents you're interested in working with.

These should be new agents you don't currently have a relationship with and aren't sending you any business.

Chances are you already have a few of these in mind. If so, great— get them on the list.

You probably need more though, so let's dive right into how to find them.

The way you identify Realtors® that are "Worth Helping A Little Extra" is by looking for agents that are actually doing business and actively marketing.

No sense in teaming up with Realtors® that don't sell and just want free stuff from loan officers.

The fact is: the good Realtors® are already taken, and they're busy.

They're not just sitting around waiting for a loan officer to come in, chat, and hand them a stack of business cards.

They're also comfortable with who they're already working with.

You're going to have to disrupt their current loan officer relationships to make something happen.

With the right approach and a solid Unique Selling Proposition, that's a lot easier than you might think.

We already know that Realtors® aren't all that loyal to loan officers, *which works to your advantage when you're on the offense.*

When it comes to their LO relationships, agents are often thinking, "What have you done for me lately?"—leaving the door wide open for you to swoop in.

(Remember, they're the ones usually dishing out the referrals, so this sense entitlement isn't altogether unwarranted.)

Before we go any further, let's reexamine why the loyalty issues exist between Realtors® and loan officers.

Think about it... This LO comes in with a box of donuts. That one has a fruit basket—everyone has "great rates and service, with excellent communication skills, quick turnaround time, and thorough follow-up procedures..."

Do you see where I'm going with this?

Question: what's your USP for a Realtor®?

Say a new producing agent is standing in front of you right now; what's your pitch?

How do you move past the usual (awkward) nonsense and get them to hear you out?

Will you win them over and get them excited about working with you?

I should be able to shake you out of your sleep at 2:00 AM and you knock that out of the park every single time.

And don't get caught up in the hype of an in-house loan officer. That's a nonissue.

I talk to in-house loan officers all the time, and they usually can't figure out for the life of them how they're sitting on the floor with 20+ agents and they're getting hardly any business out of it.

It all comes back to agents being comfortable with who they're already working with.

Another fact is that, like loan officers, agents change brokerages all the time.

When a producing agent switches companies, they usually keep their entourage, including loan officers they've been working with... assuming those LOs are doing a good job on the loans and answering the phone when the agent or their clients call.

(By the way, I hear agents gripe all the time that LOs don't answer the phone—that's an easy way to separate yourself from other loan officers. Answer the phone!)

These are the reasons why you need a bullet proof USP.

We'll cover your USP shortly, but first, let's talk about finding the right agents so you can put your new USP to use and start making some money.

Good WHALE Hunting: Finding <u>NEW</u> Producing Agents

Preparation is key. You don't want to waste time talking to and chasing Realtors® that have nothing to bring to the table.

Rather, spend time up front researching and finding the right agents to approach.

For this next part—building your lead list of Realtors®, adding notes, etc.—having a good CRM will be incredibly helpful.

If you don't have a CRM, use an Excel or Google Docs spreadsheet.

Producing agents are not hard to find, and there are a lot of ways you can go about it.

One of my favorites is to use the search engines just like a consumer would.

More often than not, you'll see producers at the top of search engines for phrases like "CITY real estate" and "CITY homes for sale".

If an agent has a website that's on the first or second page of Google or Bing for highly competitive real estate search phrases, whether it's an organic listing or a paid ad, they're doing more than the average real estate agent to promote their business.

Not to mention they're getting plenty of traffic as a result.

You'll have to sift through the mega sites like Realtor.com, Zillow, Trulia, Homes.com, etc. (we'll talk about how to use these sites as well) to find the individual agent websites, but they're definitely there if you dig just a little bit...

Especially when you make your way to pages 2 and 3, which isn't optimal placement, but still pretty good considering we're talking about highly competitive real estate key phrases and Realtors® that are going toe to toe with giant national real estate portals for search engine placement.

You can find these agents all over for any city or geographic area you're interested in targeting.

Some of the most popular real estate search phrases are:

- ▶ CITY real estate
- ▶ CITY real estate listings
- ▶ CITY homes for sale
- ▶ Homes for sale in CITY
- ▶ CITY condos
- ▶ CITY condos for sale
- ▶ CITY realtor
- ▶ CITY real estate agent
- ▶ Search CITY real estate
- ▶ Search CITY homes for sale

Simply replace "CITY" with your city, town, county, or community of interest, and test searches including a reference to state or state abbreviation (i.e.— "San Diego, CA homes for sale") where applicable to pull up search results with Realtor® websites that are getting traffic to them.

Many of the results will be larger Brokerage websites (which may or may not be a good option for you—set these aside for later), and also, major real estate search portals.

These major real estate portals can provide you with direct access to their advertisers—agents that are spending money on marketing.

You can do similar research directly on these real estate portal websites (Zillow, Trulia, Realtor.com, Homes.com, etc.)

Same idea—just run some searches and take note of the Realtors® that are paying for premium advertising listings.

Now, obviously just because an agent is paying for premium placement doesn't mean they're a good fit for you (or a producer for that matter), but it shows that they're investing in their business, which is a good starting point.

Keep in mind: this strategy is not about paying for their marketing. Instead, you're going to piggyback off of *their* marketing efforts. To do that, you need to provide a lot of value. We'll get into that momentarily.

Another strategy to help you determine which Realtors® are worth approaching is looking at their track record by checking information available through the MLS.

This includes number of sales for the year, listing inventory, length of time their listings are on the market, and other helpful information you can access.

You can also find proactive agents that are marketing and driving traffic through social media, videos on YouTube, Craigslist, email marketing, etc.

There's also no shortage of agents that are consistently spending money on traditional advertising, which you can spot all over your local market.

These are all agents you could be helping generate more business— that's the key.

Good WHALE Hunting: Eligibility Checklist

Once you've come up with a list of 25+ new WHALE candidates, you're going to stack-rank these agents based on the perceived opportunity they present, and productivity—your A's, B's, & C's.

Of the 25+ potential WHALE agent partners, your goal is to partner up with 3-5 of them, no more than 10.

Each of these agents should be in a position to send you at least 1, possibly 2 new clients every 30-60 days.

Add these agents to your CRM, along with their contact info, website address, LinkedIn profile URL, Facebook business page URL, and other details you uncover that may be helpful to have at your fingertips.

You're also going to want to grade your potential relationship with them on a level from 1-5 (5's are your best friends)—do this after your first phone call and/or meeting based on how the conversations go, and keep this score current as your relationship develops.

Other helpful information to look at before you start reaching out to agents:

If they have their own website (which is an important indicator of a more serious agent), look for the following:

> ► **What kind of mortgage information are they offering on their website?**
>
> Most Realtor® websites have very weak mortgage content, often times linking to 3rd party websites like Zillow or Mortgage 101, which basically *hijack* their traffic and do nothing to help the Realtor® generate qualified leads for themselves.
>
> That, or they have an intimidating pre-qual form that goes for the jugular, which is ineffective from a lead

generation standpoint and doesn't convert leads for them.

Same goes for a mortgage calculator. If that's all they have, they're not going to generate any business from it.

Or they have nothing for mortgage at all, which means people have to leave their website and venture off on their own to go find that information. Once a potential client leaves their site, they're not coming back.

That gives you a chance to explain the disadvantages of this kind of setup, while offering a solution to patch the hole + help them generate pre-approved buyer leads by replacing their busted (or altogether missing) mortgage content with a mortgage lead generation landing page that captures qualified leads for both you and the agent...

Basically, doing the same thing Zillow, Trulia, and all the other big dog real estate technology companies are doing to convert visitors into qualified pre-approval leads.

You're not necessarily going to start out conversations with new agents talking about this right out the gate, but that's where this is headed, and knowing whether a Realtor® will be a good candidate for this kind of partnership is key.

Your goal is to find strong agents that are doing marketing with websites that you can plug your lead generation landing pages into.

This will help them get better results from their marketing efforts and generate exclusive leads for both you and the Realtors® you're partnering with.

Also, the more pre-approved buyers an agent has in their database, the more ammunition they'll have when going into listing presentations and convincing sellers that they're the Realtor® for the job when it comes to selling homes.

More pre-approved buyers = more exposure = more showings = more competitive offers = higher bids = more homes sold quicker and for more money.

More buyers = more sellers.

Sellers are future buyers... And so it continues.

► **How is the Home Search setup on their website?**

Knowing what the agent is using to capture homebuyer leads for home searches will help you figure out their strengths/weaknesses when it comes to lead generation.

Play around with their home search tool.

Is there any lead generation ability like a "register to search" form before you start searching?

Is it just an open/free search where you can look at properties and the Realtor® gets nothing out of it?

Is it a delayed lead capture pop-up that appears after you run a couple searches and try to look at listings?

Not having any lead capture is the worst type of setup, followed by a register to search right up front that just goes for the jugular.

The most effective of the 3 is the delayed pop-up, which can generate a lot of leads, but lead quality is usually an issue as many people put in bogus information just to bypass the form.

As a mortgage professional, having home search landing pages that you can plug into your own website and marketing, and that you can offer to partner agents to use in their marketing, will further separate you from your competition, and once again, allow you to ride the coattails of your partner agents' marketing efforts while generating leads for both you and your select WHALE Realtors®.

Using a home search landing page that advertises exclusive property lists, like hot investment opportunities, foreclosures, pocket listings, homes qualified for zero down financing, etc. can further create value for homebuyers that might not be excited about a "standard" home search offer.

► **How is the Home Values Estimate page setup on their website?**

Similar to a home search landing page, as a mortgage pro, you can use a home values landing page in your own marketing, and also, offer one to Realtor® partners to help them generate more leads.

When analyzing the home values lead generation strategy of a potential WHALE partner's website, here's what to look for:

How easy is it to find? Is it one of dozens of buttons, links, and options that gets lost in the shuffle, or is there a big, bold CTA button that pulls you into the "Home Values" section right away?

Do they have a professional looking, standalone home values landing page that asks for some pertinent home information before asking for more sensitive information, like contact info... ?

Or is it a clunky form nested into the website that goes right for the "jugular" and starts out by asking for contact info, home address, and then a bunch of other questions, with red asterisks and other information all around competing for attention?

The former might be good. The latter is weak, and presents yet another opportunity for you to help a newly found WHALE agent get better results and more listings from their marketing efforts.

You will learn more about how well their current page is working for them when you speak with them.

► **Who built their website?**

A lot of Realtors® use real estate website template companies, many of which have thousands of real estate agent clients all over the country.

Most of these companies "brand" their websites with a link and/or text, or an image, at the bottom of all of their websites...

This can make their clients very easy to find, which can be another prospecting method for you to recruit agents.

For example: say you have success with a couple Realtors® that are using the same website platform.

You know that it's really easy to plug your landing pages into those websites and they have crappy stock mortgage info built into all of them—that's a prime opportunity.

Now you want to find more agents in your local market that are using that same website platform to pitch about your marketing and lead generation system that can help them get more leads and better results from their marketing...

All you need to do is run some specific Google searches that include the tagline that specific website company puts on all of their websites + the geographic area you want to find agents in, and Google will pull up every website in its directory that matches that criteria.

Knowing who built an agent's website can be helpful in determining what kind of flexibility they have in customizing their website.

Some are very easy to edit and customize, others are more restrictive.

You'll get familiar with a few of them and know exactly what you can/can't do next time you spot an agent using that website platform.

Keeping in mind, you only need a handful of good, producing WHALE agents to send you business. You want to focus on quality over quantity. You also need to be able to support the referrals they send you.

A bonus section included at the end of this chapter will show you specific search strings to put into Google that will pull up websites for the top real estate website template companies all over the country, allowing you to pull up targeted lists of Realtors® using specific website platforms in any local area you're interested in targeting.

▶ **How many listings do they have?** _____

▶ **From what you can tell, what kind of marketing are they doing online?**
Email | Blog | Social | PPC| SEO| Video | Other

Notes: _____

▶ **And what kind of marketing are they doing offline?**

Mailers | Magazines | TV | Radio | Other

Notes: _____

Be sure to plug the agents and answers into your CRM.

Once you've organized your list, now it's time for the fun part: making first contact.

You can also get an online version of the WHALE Eligibility Checklist as a worksheet you can print up here:

www.leadPops.com/manifesto-bonus

Good WHALE Hunting: Guidelines & Script for Locking Down NEW Agents

Here's a great strategy to get your foot in the door and approach WHALEs you've never spoken with:

Introduce yourself along with a plan that includes qualified leads and technology designed to help them generate more business.

The goal is to develop relationships with the right real estate agents by providing them with qualified leads that you're generating from your own marketing efforts (all the stuff you're doing currently + the new stuff you're learning in this book)...

And helping them get *better results* and *more sales* by plugging in your mortgage and real estate lead generation landing pages into *their* marketing efforts.

That's your Unique Selling Proposition!

There is no better way to get a good Realtor® (a WHALE) fired up and differentiate yourself from other LOs than by making it clear that your goal, as their preferred mortgage partner, is to help them grow their business (without having to pay for their marketing).

Later in this chapter, I'm going to cover how to improve relationships with *EXISTING* WHALEs you've already worked with.

But first, here's the low-down on how to establish *NEW* WHALE relationships to further grow your sphere of influence and referral network.

Immediate Goals

1. Find New WHALE agents.
2. Approach these WHALE agents with real value and differentiate yourself from the other loan officers that are also trying to earn their business.
3. Establish loyal WHALE agents by bringing qualified leads to the table, while strategically cementing your business into all of their marketing efforts.

Passion and conviction are the keys to success on any open.

Be sure to use voice inflection!

Good WHALE Hunting: Open Script for New Agents

This can be used on a cold call or in person.

► Have a genuine desire to help your WHALE agents.

► Ask good questions and be an excellent listener.

► Don't oversell on the open.

► Set the solid appointment.

"Hello _____, this is _____."

"I came across your website _____?" (OR –I came across your information on _____?)"

"Great, well _____, let me cut to the chase. I'm actually a loan officer/mortgage broker with _____."

"I compete with the loan officers you're currently working with."

That last line sets the tone for the rest of your conversation.

Instead of shying away from the primary objection (they've already got loan officers they're working with), you're tackling it head-on.

By saying you compete with their current loan officers, you're immediately inferring that you've got something to bring to the table that their current mortgage partners do not.

You've got their attention. Keep going.

"I'm sure most of them are nice people, but my experience is that typically LOs don't do ANYTHING to actually help their Realtor® partners grow THEIR business."

"It's like they're just kind of sitting back with their hand out waiting for referrals, and not really bringing anything to the table in return..."

You've addressed the fact that most of their current LO partners are deadbeats ☺ without bashing them, simply by saying: "I'm sure most of them are nice people..." which diffuses any sentiment that you're just talking crap about the folks that they're working with, or questioning their judgment.

Use voice inflection!

You want to convey that it boggles your mind that, in this day and age, there are still LOs out there that don't do anything to help their agents generate business!

You can pause after the last sentence and let them chime in.

This is where you'll be delighted to hear many agents cut you off and lay into their current loan officer relationships... all of a sudden, it's you and that Realtor® having a chuckle about the absurdity of loan officers expecting referrals for nothing.

"Alright, so I take a completely different approach."

"I provide my Realtors® with good leads, and also invest in tools to help my agents generate more, and <u>better qualified</u> *leads from their marketing efforts."*

"I don't have a Realtor® in your area that I'm doing this with currently..."

"All I was hoping to do today is chat with you for literally a couple minutes to learn more about your goals—what's working, what isn't—a few questions just to see if we're a good match."

"If so, we can setup another call or meet in person to discuss the details."

"So, how long have you been in the real estate business?"

Keep rolling. You don't need to ask for permission.

You're going to ask the following open-ended questions.

Get them talking about themselves (agents love doing that) and it's the perfect opportunity to learn more about how you can help them and uncover hot buttons.

Be an excellent listener. Take notes (plug them into your CRM) and look for ways to help them.

Good WHALE Hunting: Open Questionnaire

You can print this questionnaire up and take it with you if you're meeting with an agent in person (link below).

If you do that, you're going to want to get the rest of the script memorized as much as possible.

It's money. Literally. I've tested it. My mortgage clients have used it with great success. Anyone that's decent on the phone can literally take your agents from you with it, so try it out before someone else uses it on your agents.

Keep in mind: real estate agents (and people in general) love to see others taking notes as they speak, but you don't want to be reading the whole script in front of them. ☺

Once you get the answers from the agent, add them to your CRM or spreadsheet, combining their answers with your original research from the Eligibility Checklist.

To print this up, get the online version of the "Good WHALE Hunting: Open Questionnaire" here:

www.leadPops.com/manifesto-bonus

1. **What kinds of clients do you like to work with?**

   Buyers | Sellers | Investors | Expired | FSBO | Military | Relocation | Luxury | Other

   Notes: _____

2. **What's your main website address?**

   _____

   Any other websites? Y | N

   Notes: _____

3. **How many visitors do you get to your website each month?**

   _____

4. **What kind of digital marketing are you doing?**

   Email | Blog | Social | PPC| SEO | Video | Other

   Notes: _____

5. **What kind of traditional marketing are you doing?**

   Mailers | Magazines | TV | Radio | Other

   Notes: _____

6. **Of all your marketing efforts, what's currently working best for you?**

   _____

7. **How many open houses are you doing each month?**

   _____

8. **How many listings do you have?**

   _____

9. **What are some of the challenges you face in your business?**

   _____

10. **On average, how many transactions are you closing per month?**

    _____

11. **What's your goal—where would you like to be?**

    _____

12. **What are some of your other LOs doing to help you with marketing and lead generation?**

    _____

Open Script Continued (after the questions):

"Great _____, thanks for sharing. This is all really good stuff."

"Based on your answers, I definitely think this is going to be a good fit."

"In a nutshell: I use the same technology and strategies that some of the most successful companies out there are using to generate qualified buyer and seller leads..."

"I share these leads with my exclusive Realtor® partners, and I also setup my preferred agents with tools and strategies so that you can get better results and generate more leads from your marketing."

"It's the same stuff the big boys like—Zillow, Trulia, Realtor.com, Homes.com—are using to convert website visitors and anonymous clicks into actual leads."

"And the best part is: they're exclusive."

"You can't sell houses to a bunch of clicks, right?"

"Without the right lead capture technology, driving a bunch of traffic through online marketing, SEO, social media, traditional marketing efforts, etc. doesn't do anything for you."

"That's like running the A/C but leaving all the windows open! You end up losing a lot of opportunities."

"Great, _____, well the solution I'm offering can fix that for you."

"I've also got some powerful tools to help with listing presentations, which, if you're interested, we can discuss more on our next call/ meeting."

"It's not going to cost you anything, and based on everything you've told me today..."

"AS LONG AS YOU CAN SELL..."

"I can pretty much guarantee that I can help you generate additional business."

"So, _____, if that sounds good, I'd love to setup an appointment to show you exactly how it works and explain everything in more detail."

3 Action Items Talk Summary

1. What the most successful companies in the industry are doing to generate quality leads from their marketing efforts.

2. How they (your Realtors®) can use the same technology and strategy in their marketing efforts.

3. A guaranteed increase in their marketing ROI, qualified leads, and referrals.

Remember to sprinkle in some additional strategic open-ended questions along the way and get them talking about their business.

Plant seeds of value. Uncover hot-buttons and pain-points, and get them talking and thinking about the fact that, for the most part, the other loan officers they work with aren't doing ANYTHING to help them actually generate business.

While other LOs are waiting on Realtors® to send them referrals, or at best bringing them coffee and donuts, you're investing time and money into helping your agents generate more business.

Setting the Solid Appointment: Following Through on Your Open

On your next call or meeting, you're going to want to have the following lead generation landing pages ready to share with each Realtor® partner:

Real Estate Landing Pages:

- ► VIP Home Search
- ► Dream Home Finder
- ► Home Valuation

Mortgage Landing Pages:

- ► Home Purchase Qualifier
- ► Today's Mortgage Rates

These are landing pages that will be shared exclusively with each WHALE Realtor® partner to generate leads for both you and that partner agent.

Landing pages can be co-branded, just branded with the Realtor's® info, or unbranded (no logo, photo, or other branding), as long as the lead notifications that come from these pages go to <u>both</u> you and your partner agent.

Your WHALE agents will be able to use these lead generation pages in all of their marketing efforts.

Installing landing pages just about anywhere is as simple as copying and pasting a link to the desired landing page from whatever the source—their website, blog, emails, social media posts, single property websites, Craigslist, PPC campaigns, using the domain on listing signs, direct mail, and much more.

All of these conversion-optimized landing pages, and many more (32 total), are available for you to try free for 30 days at:

www.MortgageFunnels.com.

Good WHALE Hunting: Guidelines & Script for Locking Down EXISTING Agents

This approach of teaming up with agents and providing them with leads and lead generation landing pages works just as well for existing Realtors® that you've already worked with.

In fact, it's easier to call on agents you already have a relationship with (even if you've only worked with them on a deal or 2) than it is to go after brand new agents, cold.

This strategy gives you a compelling reason to call on Realtors® that you've worked with in the past and would like to get more business from, without it being an awkward (and usually pointless), "Hey you got any referrals you could send me?" type of phone call.

Usually, it's not necessarily the fault of the LO that a relationship fizzles out.

A lot of times, it's because another loan officer came into the picture and snatched away the agent by offering some sort of value above and beyond a promise to do a good job on the loan.

By the way, most Realtors® won't call to report that to you either (unless they're trying to pit you up against one another to see who can come up with the best perks, which is a red flag in terms of their character and may not be the type of agent you want to be working with).

Usually, they just become less responsive and eventually, fade away completely. Sometimes it's more abrupt than that.

Another common scenario is you've worked with an agent on just one or 2 transactions, you know they're a producer and could be sending you deals regularly, but they're not and you haven't found a good way of circling back to them and taking the relationship to a new level.

I'm sure you've also got agents you work with that do send you clients rather consistently, but you know they could be sending you more deals than they are currently, and you'd like to position yourself ahead of the other LOs that are getting that business.

Other times, a deal falls through and so does the relationship with the agent.

Or you just lose touch for no reason in particular.

And when it comes to agents that you know are sending you all the clients they can... remember: all good things come to an end.

Continuing to do a great job on the loans and answering their calls is of the utmost importance, but chances are, if they're a producer, you're still at risk of another good LO that's a strong salesperson and persistent in their pursuit of that Realtor's® business luring them away.

These are all golden opportunities and low-hanging fruit when you have the right USP.

The bottom line is you've got to go after you want.

This strategy gives you the ability to reach out to the Realtors® who you know are producers and that you've enjoyed working with, but for one reason or another, ended up losing contact with you and are currently referring their business elsewhere.

Like I said before: Realtors® aren't all that loyal to loan officers, giving you ample opportunity to bring them back into your inner circle when you've got a solid USP.

This time, by making sure the referrals are a 2-way street and helping them generate more business, it's going to be a lot harder for the next LO that comes along to steal your agents.

There is no better way to get a good Realtor® fired up and differentiate yourself from other LOs than by making it clear that your goal, as their preferred mortgage partner, is to help them grow their business by providing them with qualified leads and helping them get more sales from their marketing efforts.

The great rates, service, answering calls, communication, quick turnaround time, etc.—of course that's important too, but that's to be expected, and you should let them know that.

All of a sudden, the other LOs that are harping on those things as if they're groundbreaking offerings, never before seen or heard by anyone... seem pretty silly.

The fact is: good agents come and go. Although you can't prevent good Realtors® from working with other LOs, you can put systems in place that increase loyalty and make it a lot more difficult for other loan officers to waltz in and snatch your agents out from underneath you.

You're going to use the same WHALE Eligibility Checklist from the earlier section to stack rank your existing agents' productivity and likeability before you start reaching out.

Also, same as before, you'll want research their Facebook, LinkedIn, MLS data like number of transactions and listings, website, online marketing, offline marketing, etc. to make sure you're only focusing on agents that are worth going after.

Once you've got all that information in your CRM or spreadsheet, you'll be ready to make contact with your existing agents.

The goal for these conversations is to build stronger relationships with your agents so that you can get more referrals from Realtors® that have sent you business in the past, or are currently sending you business but could be doing more, and also, rekindling relationships with agents that have fallen by the wayside.

Good WHALE Hunting: Open Script for <u>EXISTING</u> Agents

This can be used on a cold call or in person. This script is similar, but not identical to the "New WHALE Open Script".

- ▶ Have a genuine desire to help your WHALE Agents
- ▶ Ask good questions and be an excellent listener
- ▶ Don't oversell on the open
- ▶ Set the solid appointment

"Hello _____, it's _____, with (company name)."

"How are you?"

Chat them up briefly and then cut to the chase.

"Great _____, well let me cut to the chase."

"The reason for my call is that I'm selecting a couple Realtors® locally to work with on some lead generation and marketing strategies."

"For one, I'm doing marketing in your area, which is producing some good leads that I'd like to be able to refer to an agent that I know will do a great job for my clients."

"The second part is I'm setting up my partner agents with the same lead generation technology I'm using in order to help my agents generate more, better qualified leads from their own marketing efforts."

"It's the same kind of lead gen strategy Zillow, Trulia, Realtor.com, and a lot of the other big boys are using to generate qualified leads (instead of just a bunch of tire kickers)."

"I think you'd agree that typically LOs don't do ANYTHING to actually help agents grow THEIR business."

"It's like they're just kind of sitting back with their hand out waiting for referrals; it's a one way street..."

Use voice inflection!

You want to convey that it boggles your mind that, in this day and age, there are still LOs out there that don't do anything to help their agents generate business!

You can pause after the last sentence and let them chime in.

This is where you'll be delighted to hear many agents cut you off and lay into their current loan officer relationships... all of a sudden, it's you and that Realtor® having a chuckle about the absurdity of loan officers expecting referrals for nothing.

"Alright, so I've taken a completely different approach."

"Thing is, I don't have a Realtor® partner in your area that I'm doing this with currently..."

"So _____, long story short: I sat down to make a list of who I wanted to offer this to and you're one of the first people that came to mind."

"I'm obviously not looking for an answer from you now or today..."

"And before we get into it too much further, I was hoping to chat with you literally for a couple minutes—just to learn more about you— your goals, what's working, what isn't—just a few questions to see if this is going to be a good fit."

"If so, we can setup another call or meet in person to discuss the details."

"A few minutes is all we need today."

"So, _____, remind me: how long have you been in the real estate business?"

Keep rolling. You don't need to ask for permission!

You're going to ask the same open-ended questions as before.

Get them talking about themselves—Realtors® love doing that and it's the perfect opportunity to learn more about how you can help them and uncover hot buttons.

Be an excellent listener. Take notes (plug them into your CRM) and look for ways to help them.

Good WHALE Hunting: Open Questionnaire

You can print this questionnaire up and take it with you if you're meeting with an agent in person (link below).

If you do that, you're going to want to get the rest of the script memorized as much as possible.

It's money. Literally.

Keep in mind: real estate agents (and people in general) love to see others taking notes as they speak, but you don't want to be reading the whole script in front of them. ☺

Once you get the answers from the agent, add them to your CRM or spreadsheet, combining their answers with your original research from the Eligibility Checklist.

To print this up, get your online version of the "Good WHALE Hunting: Open Questionnaire" here:

www.leadPops.com/manifesto-bonus

1. **What kinds of clients do you like to work with?**

   Buyers | Sellers | Investors | Expired | FSBO | Military | Relocation | Luxury | Other

   Notes: _____

2. **What's your main website address?**

   _____

   Any other websites? Y | N

   Notes: _____

3. **How many visitors do you get to your website each month?**

    _____

4. **What kind of digital marketing are you doing?**
    Email | Blog | Social | PPC| SEO| Video | Other
    Notes: _____

5. **What kind of traditional marketing are you doing?**
    Mailers | Magazines | TV | Radio | Other
    Notes: _____

6. **Of all your marketing efforts, what's currently working best for you?**

    _____

7. **How many open houses are you doing each month?**

    _____

8. **How many listings do you have?**

    _____

9. **What are some of the challenges you face in your business?**

    _____

10. **On average, how many transactions are you closing per month?**

    _____

11. What's your goal—where would you like to be?

_____

12. What are some of your other LOs doing to help you
with marketing and generating business?

_____

Open Script Continued (after the questions)

"Great _____, thanks for sharing. This is all really good stuff."

"Based on your answers, I definitely think this is going to be a good fit."

"As I mentioned before (and we're almost finished)..."

"I use the same technology and strategies that some of the most successful companies out there are using to generate qualified buyer and seller leads..."

"I share these leads with my exclusive Realtor® partners, and I also setup my preferred agents with tools and strategies so that you can get better results and generate more leads from your marketing."

"It's the same stuff the big boys like—Zillow, Trulia, Realtor.com, Homes.com—are using to convert website visitors and anonymous clicks into actual leads."

"And the best part is: they're exclusive."

"You can't sell houses to a bunch of clicks, right?"

"Without the right lead capture technology, driving a bunch of traffic through online marketing, SEO, social media, traditional marketing efforts, etc. doesn't do anything for you. Not like it should, anyway."

"That's like running the A/C but leaving all the windows down! You end up losing a lot of clients and opportunities."

"Great, _____, well the solution I'm offering can fix that for you."

"I've also got some powerful tools to help with listing presentations, which, if you're interested, we can discuss more on our next call/ meeting."

"It's not going to cost you anything, and based on everything you've told me today..."

"I can pretty much guarantee that I can help you generate additional business."

"You just need to be able to <u>sell</u>, which I know isn't a problem for you!"

"So, _____, if that sounds good, I'd love to setup an appointment to show you exactly how it works and explain everything in more detail."

3 Action Items Talk Summary

1. What the most successful companies in the industry are doing to generate quality leads from their marketing efforts.

2. How they (your Realtors®) can use the same technology and strategy in their marketing efforts.

3. A guaranteed increase in their marketing ROI, qualified leads, and referrals.

Remember to sprinkle in some additional strategic open-ended questions along the way and get them talking about their business.

Plant seeds of value. Uncover hot-buttons and pain-points, and get them talking and thinking about the fact that, for the most part, the other loan officers they work with aren't doing ANYTHING to help them generate business.

While other LOs are waiting on Realtors® to send them referrals, or at best bringing them coffee and donuts, you're actually investing time and money into helping your agents generate more business.

Set the Solid Appointment: Following Through on Your Open

On your next call or meeting, you're going to want to have the following lead generation landing pages ready to share with each Realtor® partner:

Real Estate Landing Pages:

- ▶ VIP Home Search
- ▶ Dream Home Finder
- ▶ Home Valuation

Mortgage Landing Pages:

- ▶ Home Purchase Qualifier
- ▶ Today's Mortgage Rates

These are landing pages that will be shared exclusively with each WHALE Realtor® partner to generate leads for both you and that partner agent.

Landing pages can be co-branded, just branded with the Realtor's® info, or unbranded (no logo, photo, or other branding), as long as the lead notifications that come from these pages go to <u>both</u> you and your partner agent.

Your WHALE agents will be able to use these lead generation pages in all of their marketing efforts...

Installing landing pages just about anywhere is as simple as copying and pasting a link to the desired landing page from whatever the source—websites, blogs, emails, social media posts, single property websites, Craigslist ads, PPC campaigns, using the domain on listing signs, direct mail, and much more.

All of these conversion-optimized landing pages, and many more (32 total), are available for you to try free for 30 days at:

www.MortgageFunnels.com.

Overcoming Possible Objections

I'm going to state the obvious: not every agent you pitch is going to become a partner.

However, through the strategic prospecting outlined in this chapter, and knowing common hot buttons and pain points going into these conversations, you're going to greatly increase your chances of converting agents you want to work with into a strategic partners and referral sources.

Preparing for questions and possible objections will further help you in your efforts to grow your Realtor® base, so I'm including the top questions and objections along with scripts to help you overcome them.

As with all sales, these objection handlers won't all work on everyone, but if you're talking to the right agents, they definitely will help you flip those whose knee jerk reaction is to object or reject any new loan officer who tries to pitch them.

1. I already have loan officers I'm working with.

"Hey awesome. I understand. All of my agents have other LOs they're working with. I totally expect that."

"And that's actually why I called you."

"In my experience, most LOs want referrals from agents... but they hardly ever reciprocate. I think that's outrageous."

"I approach it the other way around."

"I bring my agents good leads that I generate, and help them get more leads out of their marketing, so I'm really selective about who I partner with."

"By the looks of it, you seem like the type of agent I like to work with, so I'm just looking to throw my hat in the ring and see if there's a match."

IF YOU HAVEN'T ASKED THIS YET—

"What are some of your current LOs doing to help you generate business?"

"How is that working out in terms of generating leads?"

IF YOU ALREADY ASKED THE QUESTIONS ABOVE, JUMP TO—

"As I mentioned, I'm generating leads in _____ (city or community) and I'd love to develop a relationship with a <u>good</u>, reliable agent in the area so that I can refer these leads out and know they're getting taken care of."

"You don't have to change a thing."

"I just need to know if you have the bandwidth to handle extra business at this point."

"How does that sound?"

2. I don't know how to plug these landing pages into my website.

"Not a problem. It's super easy."

"All we're doing is basically copying and pasting links to the landing pages in strategic areas of your website to make sure that potential clients that are coming on here aren't slipping through the cracks."

"It's a simple copy and paste to get them on there, and it's just as easy to remove them at any point if you decide you want to go a different direction."

"I can help you with it if you provide me with the login."

"I've got a techy assistant that can plug these in for us in like 15-20 minutes tops."

"If you like it and you see results, we'll keep 'em on there. If not, we'll take 'em off."

"I do recommend trying it out for at least 60-90 days to give them a chance to start producing."

"Some of my partners see results the day we go live, sometimes it takes a few weeks."

"It depends on your marketing and current traffic."

IF NEEDED—

"You can also have your assistant or web company do it."

"I'll supply the links, we just need to tell them where to plug them in. I can help with that too."

3. What if I want to remove the landing pages?

"Great question."

"I have a hunch that once you start seeing the leads come in, the last thing you're going to want to do is remove these pages!"

"However, if you decide you want to remove them, taking them off is as easy as it is to add them."

"Simply login and remove the links, or point the links somewhere else. I can help you with that too."

"So far, none of my partner agents have asked me to do this, but if you do, I'll be more than happy to comply, of course."

4. Is this RESPA compliant?

"Definitely. First off, I'm sending you leads because these people need help from a real estate agent. I'm not a real estate agent."

"You're not obligated to send me referrals in return."

"Whether or not you add me to your LO rotation is up to you. If you do decide to refer me clients, I'll be honored and I'll take great care of anyone you refer me."

"Something else to consider in terms of RESPA compliance is that I'm paying for the landing pages and conversion optimization tools, but you're still paying for your website and marketing."

"If you want to take it a step further, I've broken it down to where each of these landing pages costs me $X per month."

"I'm providing you with X number of pages, so how about this: we do a 90 day agreement."

"For the 90 days, you pay me $X for the landing pages, and if at the end of 90 days, we decide it's a good fit and want to continue, we do another 90 days."

"Obviously the system costs me a lot more than I'm charging you for it, but you're only going to pay for the portion you're using."

"If for some reason, at any point, we decide it's not a good fit, we'll go ahead and cancel the agreement and I'll reimburse you the full amount."

EXAMPLE OF HOW THIS WORKS—

Most landing page systems cost under $200/month.

Let's say for $200/month, you get up to 100 landing pages.

That's $2 per landing page/month.

If you give each Realtor 5 landing pages, that's $10 per month.

Over 90 days, that's $30 they owe you.

Ask for a check. Take them out to dinner to discuss the marketing plan and pay for the meal.

Note the opinions above do not constitute legal advice and I recommend that you consult with an attorney if you have questions about how to comply with RESPA.

5. I don't like the idea of plugging your links into my website.

"Thanks for being candid with me about that. No problem."

"What are some of your concerns?"

"Anything else?"

SEE IF ANY OF THEIR CONCERNS ARE COVERED IN THIS SECTION, THEN ADDRESS THEM ONE BY ONE—

"There are a lot of other ways you can use these pages besides plugging them into your website, but keep in mind: your website is the hub of all your marketing, so if that's not optimized to convert leads, everything else will suffer."

"A few other ways my agents are using these pages is in email marketing, social media, listing signs—you can plug them in anywhere!"

6. I'm busy enough as is.

"I love it. That's usually a great problem to have!"

"A lot of my best agents told me the exact same thing when we first started working together."

"Let me ask you this: does that mean if I send you pre-approved buyers and serious sellers, you'd have to turn them away?"

"If I could help automate some of the follow up on buyer leads so that you're not wasting time with tire-kickers and people that aren't qualified, would that be of interest?"

"Is it an issue with lead quality—wasting time with too many leads that aren't qualified?"

"A lot of my best agents have found that they're getting bogged down by crappy leads... quantity isn't a problem, it's the quality..."

"I'm not going to be wasting your time with people that aren't serious."

"How are you getting your leads currently?"

7. Will you pay for some marketing?

"That's not typically something I do since I'm paying for the landing pages and lead conversion tools, but we can discuss it, definitely. It also, of course, depends on the marketing."

"And the <u>ONLY</u> way I'd do that is if we plug the holes in your website and other areas that are missing lead conversion tools."

"Without that, it's pointless for <u>either</u> of us to pay for marketing."

"Right now, you've got a website that has very little chance of converting <u>qualified</u> leads."

"It looks nice, but it's not optimized for lead generation."

"If I'm going to do any co-marketing with you, we need to fix that ASAP."

"Otherwise, it's like me coming over to hang out at your house and you asking me to pay for half of the A/C bill, but when I look around, you've got all the windows and doors open."

"Sure, if I'm going to hang out for a while, I'll help you pay for the A/C bill... but FIRST we're going to need to go around and close the windows and doors to make sure we're <u>both</u> getting something out of it. Make sense?"

8. Where else can I use these landing pages?

"I'm glad you asked! Anywhere and everywhere!"

"What's your next marketing campaign?"

"Are you doing any email blasts or social media posts in the near future?"

"Besides your website, I recommend we plug them into blog posts, single property websites, listing signs and open house signs, email blasts, email newsletters, direct mail, social media ads, Craigslist, TV and Radio ads, webinars, events, door hangers, your email signature, your voicemail message—you name it!"

"I recommend we start with your website, since that's the hub of all your marketing, but then we look at plugging them into some of the other things you're doing to make sure it's all optimized to convert leads and you're not missing out on clients."

9. Who gets the leads?

"We both do."

"They're exclusive to us. I set it up so that as soon as a lead comes through, we're both notified instantly via email."

"I can also set up a text message alert to your cell phone if you want."

10. Who follows up with the leads?

"We can do it either way."

"Most of my agents want me to follow up with the buyer leads, that way you're not wasting time with people that aren't qualified."

"I get them pre-approved and send them back to you as soon as they're ready."

"Keep in mind: we'll <u>both</u> get the notifications as soon as a lead comes through, so you know about every single lead, but typically I follow up and make sure they're serious before handing them off to you."

"For the seller leads, I'd recommend <u>you</u> follow up, and I can step into the picture when it comes time to getting them pre-approved for their next home."

"One thing you'll also find about me is I ANSWER THE PHONE. Communication between my agents, clients, and I is definitely one of my strong suits."

Finding Realtors® with Websites Built by Specific Website Providers

Earlier in this chapter, I covered how to find Realtors® using some general searches on Google and the large real estate portal websites.

That works well, but you've got to sift through the results to find the agents that have websites.

Here's another prospecting strategy for you that yields <u>nothing but</u> agents with their own websites...

There are a lot of real estate website template companies out there.

Many of them have hundreds, thousands, and in some cases, tens of thousands of Realtor® clients... all with nearly identical websites.

That makes their clients easy to find—if you know what you're doing.

The good news is: even if you don't, I do.

I'm going to share with you how to strategically target Realtors® in YOUR market that are using some of the most popular real estate website companies out there.

A few advantages of targeting Realtors® with websites include:

▶ Most of them are full-time and more serious about their business than agents who just have a page of their broker's website.

▶ Most of them are doing marketing and trying to generate leads.

▶ Most of them have mortgage content on their website, which typically does nothing for them at best, and actually hijacks their traffic at worst.

▶ Once you get your landing pages onto one of their sites, showing other agents with the same website provider how it works is even easier.

The key to successfully prospecting Realtors® online is in having a basic understanding how search engines work.

Each search engine will produce different results, so if you plug the same search phrase into Google and then Bing, you will know you have "exhausted" a search phrase and can move to a new one.

Using Trigger Words/Phrases

There are "trigger words/phrases" that you can add to just about any search string that will define your search results and help you find prospects you would not have found otherwise.

Whenever you type in a specific search phrase and you're looking for an <u>exact match</u> of that phrase, such as—Mortgage Center—you must place that phrase in quotes— "mortgage center"—in order to yield an exact match (whether or not you use capital letters doesn't matter).

If the segment of the search string is only one word (or has no spaces), for example—Apply—you don't need to use quotes.

Here are some examples of trigger words and phrases:

- ▶ "Apply Now"
- ▶ "Apply Online"
- ▶ "Apply Today"
- ▶ "Branch Manager"
- ▶ Financing
- ▶ "First Time Homebuyer"
- ▶ "Get Pre-Approved"
- ▶ "Home Search"
- ▶ "Home Sellers"
- ▶ "Loan Application"
- ▶ "Loan Officers"
- ▶ "Mortgage Application"
- ▶ "Mortgage Calculator"
- ▶ "Mortgage Center"
- ▶ "Our Team"
- ▶ Relocation
- ▶ "Search for Homes"
- ▶ Staff
- ▶ "Staff Directory"
- ▶ "Your Home's Value"

You can also use large brokerage names to find agents with a specific agency:

- ▶ "Better Homes and Gardens"
- ▶ "Century 21"

- "Coldwell Banker"
- ERA
- "Exit Realty"
- "Keller Williams"
- RE/MAX
- "Realty Executives"
- Sotheby's
- Weichert

To define geographic targets to include in your search strings, include one of the following:

- Area Code
- City
- City, State
- State
- Zip Code

To attach search strings together, use a plus (+) sign. This will produce results that match your specific criteria of websites that ONLY include your trigger words/phrases + a reference to, for example, the city or state you're targeting.

Real Estate Website Companies

Many real estate website providers brand their websites with phrases like "Website Built by _____", which makes it easy to find their clients.

You literally copy and paste the phrase into Google (in quotes) + any city or state you want to target and there you go—a list of every Realtor® in that area using that specific website template provider.

The following is a breakdown of some of the largest real estate website template providers in the US, along with search strings on how to find their clients.

Keep in mind: including trigger words/phrases within these searches allows you to create even more customized and specific results.

One last thing: I'd include examples of these websites, however, most agents change website providers every 1-2 years, so including URLs is pointless as the website providers are not going to stay the same, and if anything, would create confusion.

The good news is: adding your landing pages to any of these websites is a matter of copying and pasting links on the desired pages. All of these sites are customizable and ALL OF THEM need conversion optimization.

Tips:

- ▶ Replace the references to "STATE" with an actual state, city, or zip code you want to target.
- ▶ Add additional trigger words/phrases to any of the search strings below to get more specific results.
- ▶ At the end of the list, I'm going to give you a link to a web page so you can just copy and paste these search strings right into Google.

Agent Advantage (Homes.com)

Search Strings:

"Homes Media Solutions" + "mortgage calculator" + STATE

"Powered by Homes.com" + STATE

/MortgageCalc.aspx + homes.com + STATE

Agent Image
Search Strings:

"Design by Agent Image" + STATE

"Agent Image" + "mortgage calculator" + STATE

AgentWebsite.net
Search Strings:

AgentWebsite® + "property organizer" + STATE

"Web Hosting by AgentWebsite®" + STATE

BoomTownROI
Search Strings:

boomtown + financing + "what's my home worth" + STATE

"is a team of local real estate experts ready to reveal the secrets of how we can help you sell your home. From setting the price to creating marketing campaigns" + STATE

Tip: the entire paragraph above is "stock" on these websites, so by placing the entire text in quotes and running a Google search, you will pull up all the websites that have that exact same paragraph on them.

Craig Proctor Systems (Consulnet)

Search Strings:

"owned by ConsulNet Computing" + STATE

"craig proctor" + "Buy with ZERO Down" + STATE

----

iHomeFinder

Search Strings:

"Powered by iHomefinder" + STATE

----

iHomefinder + /valuation-form/ + STATE

LinkURealty

Search Strings:

"Powered by LinkURealty" + STATE

LinkURealty + "VIP Home Request" + STATE

MarketLeader

Search Strings:

"Powered By Market Leader" + STATE

"The quality of a school can greatly influence home values in an area. As a local expert" + sell + STATE

PipelineROI (a la mode)

Search Strings:

"Another website by PipelineROI" + "looking to buy" + STATE + "home search"

"Another website by PipelineROI" + "looking to buy" + "your home's value" + STATE

Tip: a la mode has mortgage, appraiser, and home inspector clients, as well... avoid those by using more specific searches, like those including a brokerage name in the example below...

One more example search string:

"Another website by PipelineROI" + california + "keller williams"

Placester

Search Strings:

"Real Estate Marketing by Placester" + STATE

"Powered by Placester" + STATE

"Real Estate Advertising by Placester" + STATE

Point2Agent

Search Strings:

Point2Agent + "how much can you afford" + STATE

"The correct selling price of a home is the highest price that the market will bear. To assist you in determining the correct asking price" + STATE

Real Estate Webmasters

Search Strings:

"Real Estate Webmasters" + STATE

"Listings Site Map" + "Search MLS" + STATE

RealGeeks

Search Strings:

"Address Search" + "Interactive Map Search" + "IDX Real Estate Websites by" + STATE

"How much is your home worth?" + "... get instant property value now!" + "advanced search" + STATE

Real Pro Systems

Search Strings:

"Real Pro Systems" + /Buyer-Resources/Loan-Analysis + STATE

"Real Pro Systems" + "homes for sale" + STATE

Superlative

Search Strings:

Superlative + "homes for sale" + STATE

Superlative + /dream-home-finder.html + STATE

Top Producer

Search Strings:

"powered by TOP PRODUCER" + STATE

"TOP PRODUCER" + /home_values.asp + STATE

WebsiteBox

Search Strings:

WebsiteBox + "get a free home evaluation" + STATE

WebsiteBox + buyers + sellers + communities + "search homes" + STATE

Wolfnet

Search Strings:

"Website Service by WolfNet Technologies" + STATE

"WolfNet Technologies" + "What's Your Home Worth?" + STATE

Z57

Search Strings:

Z57 + "homes for sale" + STATE

---

z57 + "your home's value" + STATE

----

z57 + "mortgage center" + STATE

----

z57 + /prequalify.shtml + STATE

Zillow

Search Strings:

"our coverage areas" + "Zillow, All rights reserved" + STATE

"Compare Mortgage Rates" + "Zillow, All rights reserved" + texas + "SEARCH FOR HOMES"

Extra:

Find websites with Zillow's "Zestimate" tool:

"Home Value Estimate" + zestimate + "Another address?" + STATE

To get all of these search strings online so you can simply copy and paste any of them right into Google, go to:

www.leadPops.com/find-agent-websites

PART 2

Your Next 275 Days & Beyond

CHAPTER 13

Recruit 2-3+ New Builder Partners

G ood builders, like Realtors®, are in a position to send you a lot of mortgage business.

Not only do new homes need financing, but also home renovation and improvement projects are prime opportunities for you to help builders get paid for their projects with refinances and 203k loans.

As with Realtors®, the key to developing strong builder relationships is bringing value to the table, above and beyond promising to do a good job on the loan.

Tactics for finding good builders, how to approach them, and methods for establishing loyal partnerships are very similar to the Realtor® co-marketing strategies provided in Chapter 12 (with some very slight tweaks)...

Hook them up with leads, and provide them with some landing pages to help them get more out of their marketing efforts.

It's a simple, effective pitch that you can use to create better relationships and more loyal referral partners.

CHAPTER 14
Twitter & LinkedIn

As a mortgage pro, know that you're not going to get anywhere near as much out of Twitter as you will out of Facebook. If you're only going to do one, make it Facebook.

If you want to keep a presence on both, great, but keep up with it, otherwise having a ghost town Twitter profile is pointless and it doesn't make sense to be linking up an empty Twitter profile to stuff like your website, email signature, etc.

LinkedIn is great for B2B marketing and keeping in front of your sphere of influence. I recommend being proactive on LinkedIn and continuing to grow your network.

In Chapter 34, you'll find a social sharing tool that enables you to post to multiple social networks at once, making it easier to stay on top of posting to various social websites, like Facebook, Twitter, LinkedIn, etc.

Twitter

Twitter marketing is similar to Facebook marketing, but you're limited to 140 characters at a time for your tweets (posts).

Like Facebook, having a large, engaged following on Twitter can help your exposure and establish you as an authority in your market.

The same tactics apply in terms of what you should be marketing—real estate tweets will always get more interest than anything mortgage-based.

Best Times to Tweet Based on 2016 Data Collected by CoSchedule.com:

- ▶ Mondays through Fridays, 12:00 PM - 3:00 PM
- ▶ Wednesdays, 5:00 PM - 6:00 PM

Bonus: For more information on Twitter and how it works, go to:

www.leadPops.com/manifesto-bonus

LinkedIn

With over 400 million users worldwide, and over 100 million in the US, LinkedIn is the ultimate B2B social network.

Make it a point to connect with as many business partners in your network as you can, including: Realtors®, builders, CPAs, attorneys, insurance agents, title reps, home stagers, home decorators, landscapers, listing photographers, home inspectors, appraisers, escrow agents, architects, and all other professionals you work with, or simply know and have a relationship with.

You'll also find that many of your clients/borrowers are professionals with profiles on LinkedIn, so don't overlook using LinkedIn as another way to connect with and stay in front of your customers, past and present.

Posting value-added, business-related, and industry-specific information regularly on LinkedIn can help you keep in front of these connections and stay top of mind, while further establishing you as an expert and thought leader in your market.

Don't post stuff that should be on Facebook on LinkedIn.

Best Times to Post on LinkedIn According to LinkedIn:

LinkedIn says, "Our busiest hours are morning and midday, Monday through Friday The best times to post include:"

Tuesdays:
7 AM – 8 AM, 10 AM – 11 AM, 12 PM, and 5 PM – 6 PM

Wednesdays & Thursdays:
7 AM – 8 AM, 12 PM, and 5 PM – 6 PM

Also note: the more complete your profile, the better your chances of getting profile views and growing your network, so be sure to have a professional photo, and fill out your summary, past work experiences, and skills.

Bonus: For more information on LinkedIn and how it works, go to:

www.leadPops.com/manifesto-bonus

CHAPTER 15

Use Powerful Online Mortgage Rate Tables

I f you're competitive with rates and want to generate your own exclusive mortgage leads, some great traffic sources are online mortgage rates tables.

Plugging into a rate table is like turning on a traffic machine where the hard work of figuring out how to get the right traffic at a reasonable cost per click (CPC) has already been figured out for you.

The clicks can be expensive, but the traffic is solid, so leads usually come in at a profitable cost per funded loan.

I've worked with a lot of mortgage professionals over the years that are quite successful using rate tables as a way to generate their own exclusive mortgage leads.

I'm not a fan of the lead-slinging tactics used by many of these companies, however, their rate tables have proven to be a viable source of business for a lot of loan officers and mortgage brokers, so I will share them with you for that reason.

Here are the top rate tables in the mortgage industry:

- ▶ Bankrate, a leadPops partner company
- ▶ Clicks.net

- ▶ Homes.com
- ▶ Informa
- ▶ Katch
- ▶ Loan Explorer
- ▶ Quinstreet
- ▶ Rate Marketplace
- ▶ Realtor.com
- ▶ Zillow

The leadPops team works with many of these companies regularly.

For a list of these rate table websites online, go to:

www.leadPops.com/mortgage-rate-tables

CHAPTER 16
Target Niche Loans

There are a ton of niche markets within the mortgage space you can target effectively with social media ads, targeted lists, and partnerships with other professionals that cater to the same niche.

To go after a niche, create a microsite focused on providing information on the topic, and most importantly—tied into a landing page to capture leads.

A microsite is a mini website, typically with 3-5 pages or sections, which functions as a separate entity and lives outside of the main company homepage and/or brand URL.

Microsites are built to complement online and/or offline marketing activity.

They are similar to landing pages in that they're primarily focused on one topic and designed to convert, but they differ in that microsites may include additional navigation links to subpages, since they are meant to hold more information about a specific product or service. This allows for multiple ways to convert a lead when a campaign is more complex.

Plug your microsite into a targeted Facebook audience or mailing list to start generating exclusive leads fast!

All you need is a domain name and a simple microsite/landing page building platform.

If you have extra domain names sitting around that aren't being used for anything, those can be ideal for using with a microsite (or straight landing page).

That way you can start monetizing the domain name instead of it not doing anything for you. You can turn traffic on/off like a spigot.

Here are some ideas for mortgage niches that you can go after:

- ► 3% Below Market Interest Rate (3-2-1 buy down)
- ► 95% Financing, No Mortgage Insurance (Lender-Paid MI)
- ► 97% Financing (Conventional 97)
- ► Beach Home Financing
- ► CalHFA Benefit Programs (California Housing Finance Agency, for first-time homebuyers)
- ► CalPERS Benefit Programs (California Public Employee Retirement System)
- ► CalSTRS Benefit Programs (California State Teachers' Retirement System)
- ► Commercial Loans
- ► Construction-to-Permanent Loans
- ► Create Microsites for Referral Partners
- ► Credit Repair
- ► Debt Consolidation
- ► Desert Home Financing
- ► Down Payment Assistance Program
- ► FHA 203k Streamline (or standard)
- ► FHA Streamline Refinance

- First Time Homebuyers (zero down, FHA, VA, USDA, 203K, grants, energy efficient, tax credits, etc.)
- FSBO (for sale by owner)
- Foreclosure Bailouts
- Foreclosures
- Foreign National Loans
- Golf Course Home Financing
- Good Neighbor Next Door Mortgage
- Hard Money Loans
- Home Values for Refinance
- Home Values for Sellers
- HomePath and HomePath Renovation
- HomeReady Mortgage
- Inherited Mortgages
- Interest-Only Payments
- Jumbo Loans
- Lake Home Financing
- Land/Lot Loans
- Loans for Doctors
- Loans for Heroes
- Loans for Teachers
- Luxury Home Financing
- Manufactured Home Financing
- Mortgage After Divorce
- Mountain Home Financing
- No Income, No Asset Verification (no doc)
- No Pay Stub, No W2, No Tax Return (VOE program)

- ▶ Non-Permanent US Residents
- ▶ Non-Prime (bad credit)
- ▶ Piggyback Mortgage
- ▶ Purchase a Home 1 Day After Short Sale (must be current on mortgage)
- ▶ REO Financing (banks' real estate owned properties)
- ▶ Refinance Rate Checker
- ▶ Renovation/Rehabilitation Loans
- ▶ Reverse Mortgage
- ▶ River Home Financing
- ▶ Single Property Websites
- ▶ Short Sale Financing
- ▶ Vacation Home Financing

… and ANYTHING else you can think of!

There are several tools out there for creating landing pages and microsites.

Some of the more popular ones are Unbounce.com and LeadPages.net. The problem with those tools is they're not specific to mortgage/real estate, so it's tough to create something effective (unless you're just trying to capture a name and email address).

My company, leadPops.com, offers a simple, yet powerful microsite and landing page building platform called PagePops with over 150 templates, and built-in funnels specifically designed for the mortgage and real estate industries.

For mortgage information on PagePops, go to:

www.leadPops.com/PagePops

CHAPTER 17

Open House
Lead Generation

Marketing at open houses can be a great strategy for building Realtor® relationships and getting in front of more homebuyers.

To generate leads at open houses, use a laptop or tablet and offer:

- ► A digital open house registration page with an incentive to sign in
- ► An online "dream home finder" wish list to keep buyers updated with properties that meet their criteria
- ► On-site pre-approvals
- ► Branded maps with all available local open houses for the weekend

You can also provide additional directional signs for the open houses and pay for a service to put them out for you (split the cost with the Realtor®).

These signs should include a call-to-action and web address offering pre-approvals to homebuyers.

I'll get more into real estate sign marketing in Chapter 18.

CHAPTER 18
Real Estate Listing Sign Marketing

T eam up with Realtors® to help them get more out of their listing signs.

"For Sale" signs sit out front of homes for weeks at a time, and are rarely optimized for lead conversion. A phone number on a listing sign is pretty ineffective.

Think about it: not only are homebuyers going to take notice as they drive around the neighborhood looking at homes for sale, but curious neighbors and other passersby will, as well.

This is a great opportunity to get more out of the signage for both you and your partner agents by offering sign riders with strong calls-to-action and a web address pointing to a pre-approval landing page urging homebuyers to get pre-approved.

You can even a link up a virtual tour of the home and combine that with your pre-approval landing page or microsite.

There are some text message-based real estate marketing signs out there that typically generate low-quality leads as the homebuyers aren't expecting a call, and you don't even have any information about them other than their cell phone number (which *can* work, but usually results in an awkward phone call that doesn't end up going anywhere).

Here's an example of a real estate listing sign rider that, when paired with an effective landing page, works to generate much more than just a phone number, getting higher quality lead for both you and your Realtor® partners:

Get Pre-Approved 24/7!
www.247Approved.com

Figure 18-1: this is an example of a real estate sign rider for generating pre-approval leads. Not an actual domain name I'm using or promoting.

Here are some additional calls-to-action that can be used on real estate listing sign riders and/or open house directional signs.

All of the domains listed below are for example purposes only.

Get Pre-Approved to Buy a House!
www.EasyApprovals.com

Want to Get a Loan to Buy a Home?
www.EasyHomeLoans.com

See the Virtual Open House 24/7!
www.[address-of-home].com

How Much Home Can You Afford?
Find Out NOW!
www.HomeAfford.com

Buying a Home?
Get Your FREE
Pre-Approval Letter NOW!
www.FreeBuyerLetter.com

Know Exactly What You Can Afford
Before You Start Searching for Homes!
www.SmartBuyersKnow.com

Looking for Open Houses?
Get a FREE Up-to-Date Local
Open House List Now!
www.MyOpenHouseList.com

FREE Home Loan Qualifier—
Get Pre-Approved TODAY!
www.LoanQualify.com

Buy a Home for ZERO DOWN!
www.BuyWithZeroDown.com

Home Grants for Homebuyers!
www.SweetHomeGrants.com

**Access Local Homes for Sale
You Won't Find Elsewhere!**
www.iHomeSpy.com

Get Your Home's REAL Value FREE!
www.247HomeValues.com

Get an Amazing Deal On a Foreclosure!
www.ForeclosureSpy.com

Here are a couple services to get signs made at a decent price (no affiliation to leadPops):

www.BuildASign.com

www.SignsOnTheCheap.com

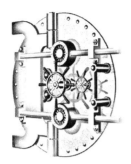

CHAPTER 19

Craigslist & Other
Free Directories

60 million people in the US use Craigslist.org each month, according to Craigslist.

In most areas, there are <u>tons</u> of homebuyers, renters, and homeowners looking for homes, financing, and other related, local services on Craigslist.

That means you can tap into that traffic and drive it to your landing pages to convert leads for cheap.

Craigslist marketing takes time and commitment, but it works and in most cases, it's free.

Another classified ads website similar to Craigslist that also gets decent traffic is www.BackPage.com (no affiliation to leadPops):

With Craigslist and most other forms of marketing, your results are only as good as your ad copy.

To become a better copywriter and learn how to craft killer headlines, get this free eBook from copyblogger:

www.copyblogger.com/copywriting-101

CHAPTER 20

Search Engine Optimization (SEO)

S earch engine optimization, or SEO, is a technique used to increase a website's organic traffic by getting prominent ranking on the search engine results pages (SERPs) for Google, Bing, and other search engines when certain keywords and phrases are typed into the search field.

Each search engine uses an algorithm based on many factors that they feel make up a good web page.

These algorithms are closely guarded by the major search engines, so no one knows exactly what they are. However, there are proven techniques that can improve your chances of ranking well in search engines for your desired keywords.

At the first mortgage marketing technology company I co-founded back in 2006, we developed template mortgage websites for thousands of loan officers and mortgage brokers nationwide.

As VP of Sales and head of product development, I devised a standardized SEO plan for our website product that resulted in over 80% of our clients placing on pages 1-2 of Google for targeted local mortgage keywords in competitive markets across the US.

Though a ton has changed in the world of SEO over the years, there are many principals and tactics that have stayed true to this day, which I'll share with you in the following sections of this chapter.

Before we go further, I'd like to make sure you know what you're in for, and set the right expectations when it comes to mortgage SEO.

In Chapter 1, I provided data that shows search volumes for mortgage vs. real estate key phrases, which reveals that mortgage SEO isn't all it's cracked up to be.

For how competitive it is and how long it takes to come up for even local mortgage key phrases (with no guarantees), the search volume just isn't there for most mortgage professionals to justify the cost and time they'd have to put into mortgage SEO.

Due to the competition, nationwide organic placement for phrases like "mortgage rates" is pretty much impossible to attain at this point, and most loan officers wouldn't want that anyway as they're only able to write loans in their home state or a handful of states they're licensed in.

That brings us to statewide key phrases, which are also incredibly competitive, with no chance of a newcomer getting organic placement for a statewide phrase like "California mortgage rates" or "California refinance" without putting at least 1-2+ years of work into building a website with great SEO architecture, usability, perpetual content creation, and ongoing quality link building.

Even with that, you wouldn't be likely to get page 1 placement for short tail key phrases (search phrases typically consisting of 1-2 keywords) considering you're competing with behemoths like Bankrate, Zillow, HSH, Homes.com, LendingTree, etc.

What's also important to know is that statewide mortgage key phrases don't get typed in all that often either.

Look at the data samples taken from SEMRush.com for May of 2018:

California Mortgage Rates:
880 Google searches per month

Refinance Rates California:
390 Google searches per month

Current Mortgage Rates California:
320 Google searches per month

Refinance California:
210 Google searches per month

California Home Loans:
210 Google searches per month

VA Loans in California:
170 Google searches per month

Those August examples accurately reflect the average number of monthly searches for those same key phrases going back to 2015.

What this tells you is that you'd be competing for top 10 placement with companies worth hundreds of millions of dollars (and some worth billions) that are pumping out fresh content daily and building new backlinks like it's nobody's business...

All for keywords that don't even get typed in enough to get the traffic you'd have to get in order to generate the leads you'd need to pay for the SEO in the first place!

Don't get me wrong, SEO can be profitable and you can place for keywords that will get you some good, quality mortgage traffic, but you've got to go into it with the right expectations and strategy...

You don't want to waste time shooting for the unattainable, or stuff that's not going to help you close more loans.

That being said, if you want to rank in Google, I recommend targeting local, long tail key phrases (longer, more specific phrases) for niche mortgage products like, "203K loans in San Diego, CA".

The fact is: anything mortgage related is going to be very competitive (even long tail key phrases at a local level), and it's still going to take a while to get first page placement, but your chances will be much better, especially if you have a domain name that you've owned for a long time that's already placing for some key phrases (even if it's on page 5).

You can work with that. A brand new domain name with no history that hasn't been indexed by Google is going to take much longer to place in the top 10 results of page 1.

In Chapter 34, I share several SEO research tools/websites that allow you to plug in any domain name to see whether it's indexed and how it's placing—which keywords it's coming up for, and what pages you'll find it on.

These tools also give you keyword data, including: search volumes, cost per click for PPC, top competitors, and much more.

SEO is a long term investment in both time and money, and realistically, (in most cases) you're not going to generate leads out of it for several months to 1 year or more, but once you place in the top 10 for relevant key phrases that are actually getting typed in by potential borrowers in your local market, you can start to see a great ROI with exclusive mortgage leads that close coming into your CRM daily as a result.

If you're still interested in pursuing SEO, more power to you. Let's continue.

Website Tag Optimization

Optimizing your website tags is one of the oldest SEO tactics, and still relevant. Having your tags setup correctly will go a long way in helping your SEO efforts.

In this section, I will help you understand how to setup your tags in a way that will give your website pages the best possible chance of showing up for your desired keywords and phrases.

First, let's decipher between the three types of SEO tags—title tags, meta tags, and description tags.

Title Tags

Title tags are the primary HTML tag elements used to describe the content of a page. They should be accurate and concise, helping search engines quickly determine what each page of a website is about. You could say they're like the titles of chapters in a book.

Websites with incorrectly worded and formatted title tags have little chance at placing well for desired searches, so it's critical to optimize your title tags if you want to rank well.

Here's what you need to know about title tags along with guidelines that will help you optimize them:

Title tags are visible in the top bar of internet browsers (Figure 20-1), and also the blue clickable text on search engines results pages (Figure 20-2).

Figure 20-1: title tags shown in Chrome's browser tab while on a website. The box with the arrow pointing at it below shows the full title tag when you place your cursor over the text in the tab.)

San Diego Home Loans & Refinance | iSanDiegoMortgage.com
isandiegomortgage.com/refinance/ ▾
Home Refinance Loans without the Hassle! Need refinancing options on a San Diego home, or other
real estate? Choosing a refinance product that matches ...

Figure 20-2: title tags shown on the search engine results page of Google as blue clickable text. The more your title tag matches up with the user's search query, the more likely they are to click-through to your website. The plain text below the green URL is the "description" tag of the page.

Title tags should include the key phrases that you want to be found for, with the most important keywords listed at the beginning.

For example: if you want to be found for "San Diego Mortgage Rates", then you want to make sure that exact phrase is included in the title tag of either your homepage or one your subpages that is focused specifically on that topic.

Title tags should match the content of each corresponding page, so again, if the title tag is, "San Diego Mortgage Rates" you need to make sure that the content of that page is about San Diego mortgage rates.

Not having them match is like writing a book with a chapter titled "How to Drive a Racecar", and then offering content about gardening... How much value would you put in a book like that?

Search engines look at the title tags and content of a website the same way since their goals is to provide relevant search results.

Something else to know is that there is a character limit to how much you can include in a title tag. There isn't an exact number, but it is widely accepted that the limit should be between 50-60 characters.

Google typically shows up to 60 characters per title tag for each listing on a SERP, or as many characters as will fit into a 600 pixel display, including as many whole words as it can before truncating it with an ellipses (...).

If you keep your titles under 60 characters, you can expect at least a majority of them to display properly.

That means you need to be concise with what you include in your title tags.

You can't just add every term you want to be found for... in fact, doing that can end up hurting you since search engines see it as "keyword stuffing".

It's important not to use the same exact title tags on various pages of your website. Repeat content is not something that search engines are fond of.

Also, don't use the same keyword multiple times within a title tag as search engines also look at that as keyword stuffing and can penalize you for it.

Meta Tags

Meta tags are another HTML element in the form of a series of keywords, separated by commas, used to support your title tag in telling the search engines what your website is about.

Meta tags cannot be seen by website visitors unless they right-click to "view source" of a page.

Optimizing meta tags was once a powerful SEO tactic, but because of abuse (people just stuffing their websites with irrelevant meta tags so they could be found for desired keywords), they have lost much of their influence, though it's still good to add relevant keywords to the meta tags of your website for the sake of not leaving them blank.

When setting up meta tags, simply use a handful of keywords that are relevant to the topic of the page you are optimizing. Don't repeat keywords within meta tag groupings on a page, and don't add too many.

There's not an exact "correct" number, but 6-12 meta tag keywords per page should be fine.

Description Tags

Description tags (also an HTML element) are the summary of a page, visible on search engine results pages as the few lines of plain text you see included with each result, beneath the blue clickable title tag text and the green URL (Figure 20-2).

Description tags are designed to give both potential visitors and search engines a quick explanation of the content of each page.

You want your descriptions to be compelling and to entice potential visitors to click into your website, not just a bunch of keywords (meta tags, as described in the prior segment, are just a bunch of keywords).

There is generally an accepted limit of around 150-160 characters per description, even though there are tons of websites that place well with longer and shorter descriptions.

Google shows up to 156 characters per description for each listing on a SERP, including as many whole words as it can before truncating it with an ellipses.

As with title and meta tags, it's very important not to just stuff your descriptions with keywords.

Here's a free tool that will help you count characters for your title tags and descriptions, and also predict how your web page will look in Google's search results:

www.moz.com/learn/SEO/title-tag

Moz is a tremendous SEO resource. Explore it.

Website Content Optimization

Ask almost any SEO expert and they'll probably agree that content is king.

That's because content is considered the single most important and powerful factor you can use to help your website get found on search engines.

Content comes in the form of informational articles, interviews, reviews, videos, images, memes, infographics, quizzes, and more.

Good content means people finding your website stay on your website for longer, and can also increase the number of other websites and blogs linking back to your website, both which are ranking factors in Google.

In the last couple of years, Google has made big changes to their algorithms to find good quality content and remove poor quality content from their search results.

Essentially, without unique, quality content, you have little to no chance at showing up for competitive mortgage key phrases in the major search engines.

Before you start writing your content (or hiring someone to do it for you), it's important to do some keyword research so that your content is targeting the best keywords that will get you the most traffic.

Keep in mind: just because certain keywords sound good to you doesn't mean people are actually searching for them.

Also, people search a wide array of keywords, so there might be quite a few that don't come to mind.

There are many websites out there that can give you an estimate of the search volume for keywords, including a free Google tool called "Keyword Planner".

Keyword Planner is mainly used for Pay Per Click advertising, but can be great for researching SEO keywords as it will give you estimates of the search volume and competitiveness of keywords, as well as suggestions of other similar popular keywords and phrases.

The link to the Keyword Planner tool is:

https://adwords.google.com/KeywordPlanner

It's very important to do your research first, since SEO can be a time consuming process. You don't want to waste your efforts on keywords that will not give you much in return.

Once you've determined good keywords, it's time to create content that will attract the search engines to your page.

Here are the key points to follow when creating your content:

- ▶ **High Quality Content**

    There is no shortcut here. Make sure your content offers real value to someone wanting to get more information on a certain topic.

    Your content needs to be engaging.

    Ask yourself, "Will people spend time actually reading this, and will they get value from it?"

    If you're unsure, share your content with knowledgeable friends, colleagues, and clients to get feedback.

    You don't have to be an expert in SEO to write good content. Assuming you're an expert in the field of mortgage, think about it as if someone came into your office and asked you for information on a specific mortgage topic... Would you be able to answer their questions?

Of course you would. With SEO content, you're just putting your expertise in writing. Your website content is a reflection of you, so make sure it demonstrates your knowledge. Keep it as simple as possible for your clients to understand (staying away from industry jargon) and the search engines will reward you for it.

► **Unique Content**

Make sure your content is unique. Copying someone else's content is not going to help your efforts. Search engines can tell if content has been taken from other sources, which will do nothing for you and will actually end up hurting you since search engines penalize websites for duplicate content.

► **Keyword Rich Content**

Referencing the keywords and phrases you're targeting throughout your content will help you rank better for them.

For example: if you are targeting "San Diego mortgage rates", make sure you use that phrase and different permutations of that phrase in your content. While this might seem obvious, it's oftentimes overlooked.

On the other hand, you don't want to go overboard. That is considered "keyword stuffing", which will hurt your rankings since search engines will see this as an effort to game the system (not to mention, keyword stuffing hurts content quality).

Think about it from your audiences' point of view: if you read something and see the same keyword/phrase used every other sentence, would you think that is well written? Search engines see content in the same way. Make sure you reference your keywords, but not to a point where it just doesn't sound right or negatively affects the readability.

▶ **Keep Your Content Fresh**

Search engines like fresh, up to date information, so if the content on your website has been the same for years, then it's time for an update. That doesn't mean you need to add new content daily. However, going through your website pages and making sure everything is current is recommended, as is creating new content on a regular (weekly or monthly) basis.

That's where having an active blog tied into your website comes into play for SEO. A blog gives you the ideal platform for adding new content to your website regularly.

Google uses an algorithm they call "Query Deserved Freshness", which rewards pages that talk about a timely topic. For example: if there is a brand new loan program in the news and you create a new page within your website for it, this page is likely to get picked up by Google quicker as it has fresh content available on that new topic.

Also, it's likely your competitors aren't jumping on opportunities like this, so search engines won't be as saturated with pages competing for this new subject.

▶ **Organize Your Content**

Instead of creating one page that talks about several loan programs or products, spread your content throughout multiple pages, giving each topic its own dedicated web page.

You can connect these pages to each other using text links with relevant keywords embedded in them, further increasing your website's crawlability and the number of pages being indexed by Google and other major search engines.

When you have too many topics/keywords on one page, you are essentially diluting the strength of that page for any of the given topics. So, when you write about a topic, dedicate one or more pages to it in order to give yourself the best chance of ranking well for corresponding keywords/phrases.

Website Architecture Optimization

While website architecture is more of a technical aspect of SEO, nonetheless, it's a vital part of the overall picture, so it's important to understand, even if only at a high level.

The structure of your website and pages is factored into how the search engines rank them.

You already know that quality content is rewarded by Google and other search engines... the same goes for websites and pages that are designed well.

Here are some of the most important areas of proper website architecture:

▶ **Site Crawlability**

When a search engine robot (also known as a "spider") visits your website, they call it "crawling" your page.

I know it sounds scary, but they're usually harmless (unless you're trying to cheat, which I'll cover along with what NOT to do later in the "SEO Mistakes" section).

Search engine spiders crawl your pages to review the information on them, so making your site easy for the spiders to crawl will ensure that they give you credit for the content and keywords within your website.

Using search engine friendly CSS code on your website will minimize the HTML code, making it cleaner and easier for the search engines to crawl your website and read your content.

Also, using text links for menu items, and creating alternative navigation paths in the footer along with breadcrumb navigation will help crawlability as well.

I recommend creating an XML sitemap that lists all the URLs from your website that you want search engines to crawl.

Spiders regularly crawl sitemaps, so by providing links to all your interior pages within the XML sitemap, you increase the opportunity for spiders to find and crawl your pages.

► **Mobile Friendly**

Make sure your website is responsive, or at least has a mobile version.

As more and more people use mobile devices to browse the internet, it's vital for SEO to have a website that works great on mobile phones and tablets.

► **Page Load Time**

Fast-loading websites rank better in search engines.

User experience is an important ranking factor, so a website that loads quickly is rewarded with better placement by Google and other search engines.

A large website size/footprint (anything over 3MB), using flash, too many images, or images that are too large, the number of external resources included in the site, page redirects, lack of compression, messy code—all of those will hurt page load times and result in lower rankings.

► Keywords in URL

As you can probably tell by now, search engines like and reward relevance. This goes for domain names and URL structure as well as website tags and content.

For that reason, including keywords in your domain name can help you place better for them.

Keywords can be included in top-level portion of the domain, for example:

"www.iSanDiegoMortgage.com" and also in the URL slugs on subpages of your website.

A URL slug is what comes after the domain extension, or the ".com" portion of the domain name.

For example: if your website domain is, "www.iSanDiegoMortgage.com" and the topic of your content page is "203K loans in San Diego, CA", you'll want to use the following structure for your domain slug on that content page:

www.iSanDiegoMortgage.com/203k-loans-in-san-diego-ca

In additional, your title, meta, and description tags should all reflect 203K loans in San Diego, CA, along with, of course, the content on that page.

► Image Optimization

Search engine spiders can't read images, so your images need to be optimized with title tags (these are also used for images) and alt tags (image tags that describe what the image is for visually impaired users, and in case the browser doesn't render the image).

For example: if your "203K loans in San Diego, CA" page has a before and after image of a home that had repairs using a 203k loan, you'd optimize that image by setting up the following:

Title Tag: San Diego 203K Loan Home Renovation

Alt Tag: Before and After 203K Loan in San Diego, CA

You'll also want to make sure your images are compressed. Large image files slow down websites, which makes for a poor user experience.

There are some free tools that reduce the file size of images without changing or reducing the quality, like www.TinyPNG.com (no affiliation to leadPops).

► **Website Security**

Search engines favor secure websites by rewarding them with a small ranking boost.

These are websites that use "https" instead of "http" in the address bar, with a green lock indicating added security.

As with the other recommendations mentioned, this is just one of many factors, and doesn't alone guarantee getting into the top 10.

Website Link Building

Building backlinks has been a major factor in SEO for about as long as search engines have been around.

When done right, backlinks are still the most powerful off-page tactic you can incorporate when it comes to increasing your search engine rankings.

Backlinks work as "votes of confidence" that search engines evaluate to see how valuable, trustworthy, and authoritative the rest of the internet views your website to be.

Not all backlinks are created equal.

Some links are more powerful than others, and there are those that can actually hurt your placement.

Link building takes strategy, time, and patience.

You're not just building links, you're building relationships, so keep that in mind when approaching a new potential back link partner and asking for their vote of confidence.

Offering compelling content and focusing on, "What's in it for them?" can go a long way in helping you get more quality links pointing back to your website.

Here are some additional guidelines to follow for building backlinks:

Link Quality

When it comes to backlinks, it's quality over quantity.

If you want to be found for "San Diego 203K loans" and you get a link pointing to your San Diego 203K loans page from a website that is considered an authority on rehab loans, that back link will be a lot stronger compared to a link from a website about dog training.

If the search engines have deemed a website as trustworthy (i.e.— it's ranking well in Google), and that website links to your page, that is a much more valuable link than, for example, a new website with no placement that links back to yours.

Concentrate on getting links back from websites and pages that are an authority and related to the keywords you want to be found for.

Quality content goes a long way in helping you build quality backlinks.

Building backlinks on spammy directory websites and link farms is considered "black hat" SEO and can get you penalized, and even blacklisted.

Anchor Text

Anchor text is the text that appears highlighted in a hypertext link and that can be clicked to open the target web page.

Diversification of your anchor text is important when it comes to link building.

In the past, Google placed more value on links with keyword rich anchor text, but as with most things related to SEO, once people figured that out, they started abusing it by creating all of their backlinks using the keywords and phrases they wanted to place for stuffed into the anchor text.

These days, over-optimizing your back link anchor text with keywords can actually get you penalized since Google sees it as trying to manipulate the system.

It's important that backlinks are natural (again, leading back to the importance of quality content—nobody wants to link to crappy or boring content), and if they're not natural (paid links—not recommended), you make them appear natural by not stuffing them with keywords.

This doesn't mean you shouldn't ever use keywords in your anchor text, but it does mean you'll want to distribute anchor text evenly across several types of link text.

Some examples of link text include:

▶ "Branded terms", for example—your name or your company's name in the anchor text

▶ "Generic anchors", like—"click here" and "this page"

▶ "Naked URLs" like— "https://iSanDiegoMortgage.com"

▶ "Titles", meaning—the title of the page or article you're building links to

You'll also want to apply these various anchor text types to the pages within your website, not just backlinks from other websites.

As mentioned before, search engines crawl your website to read your content. Better crawlability helps them give you the credit you deserve for good quality content.

You'll want text links within your content pages pointing to other content pages, as well as in your footer, breadcrumb menus, and in your sitemap.

Diversifying your anchor text within your website will also help them appear more natural vs. just stuffing additional keywords into the links of your pages.

Paid Links

Getting quality backlinks can be hard work. Naturally, there are ways to find places that sell links.

As I've said before, there are no shortcuts.

When it comes to paid links, the search engines are very aggressive at finding them, and once they identify that your link has been paid for, there is a very good chance you will receive a significant drop in your placement. Avoid paying for links for this exact reason.

Outreach

Researching websites that can offer you quality backlinks is the first step to reaching out and building relationships.

You can do this by finding websites and blogs that focus on your topic(s) of interest, reaching out via email, and asking for a back link, or even better: offering to do a guest article or blog post.

You can also find websites that link to your competitors and do the same. In Chapter 34, I offer several tools that allow you to research backlinks for any domain.

Once you have a good lead list, you can reach out via email to the website owner by doing a "who is" search on the domain name (www.nsi.com/whois) or, of course, finding contacts listed directly on the website and/or social media profiles and reaching out to them.

Remember to focus on what's in it for them!

Use a clever, intriguing subject line to get your email opened (I share awesome email open tracking software in Chapter 34), and keep it brief.

Offer some feedback. Tell them why you love their website, and how you think a link back to your content, or a guest blog post or article will help them and their audience.

Once you craft a good outreach email, you'll have a template you can use again and again. Just be sure to personalize each one at least a little bit to get better response rates.

Also, keep your local referral partners in mind as link partners. They'll be a lot easier to connect with than a cold email to someone you've never spoken with.

This goes hand in hand with creating a "Trusted Pros" referral partner directory on your website.

A "Trusted Pros" section offers you the perfect framework for adding local referral partners to your website, while giving you an opportunity to get them to link back to your website as well.

Partners such as Realtors®, builders, insurance agents, attorneys, CPAs, financial planners, title companies, home decorators, solar companies, etc. are all great candidates for featuring in your "Trusted Pros" section and building backlinks.

Social Media & SEO

I updated this section of the book in May of 2018 and as of right now, Google has said repeatedly that it does not use social media signals such as likes and comments as a ranking factor (at this point).

That doesn't mean social media can't help your search engine placement whatsoever, but it does tell you that more likes to your Facebook business page won't directly correlate to better search engine rankings for your website.

With that out of the way, let's look out how social media <u>can</u> have a positive impact on your SEO.

Social media websites place extremely well in Google for branded searches.

Look up just about any established company or individual on Google or Bing, and you'll often see their Facebook, Twitter, LinkedIn, and other social media pages placing at the top.

You can use this to your advantage and "own" more of the first page of search engines for branded keyword searches (people looking for your name and your company's name) by building up and maintaining your social profiles.

That's why it's good to market YOU, not just your company's name on everything, unless you own the company or are using a DBA (covered in Chapter 7).

The more top 10 results for your branded searches go to websites/pages that you own or have some control over, the better.

Social media pages give you plenty of opportunities to drive visitors to your website and/or blog content using links within your profile description, as well as posts, and comments.

More engagement on social media posts gives you more opportunities to drive traffic to your website, so post quality information and link back to your website often.

Traffic coming to your website is a ranking factor in Google, so not only will you get the benefit of traffic coming to your site directly from your social media pages, but also help Google see that your website is getting additional traffic, which can help it rank better.

YouTube

YouTube is owned by Google, but uses its own algorithm... it's also the second most popular search engine in the world (behind Google).

YouTube allows people to embed call-to-action links in their own videos, enabling you to use videos to drive traffic to your website, blog, and landing pages.

You can make a quick 60-90 second video on any mortgage topic and upload it to YouTube within minutes, then share that video on your website, blog, and social networks.

With the right keywords and tags embedded in the video, for example: "203K Loans in San Diego, CA", you can start placing for people looking for related information directly on YouTube as well as in Google.

Not only do YouTube videos place on YouTube and Google, but they're often shared and commented on, giving you a potential "social boost" in exposure and leads.

Facebook, Twitter, LinkedIn, and Google+

As you already know, these are incredibly popular websites that most individuals and businesses in the US are using daily.

People go to these sites to socialize, kill time, share thoughts and opinions, and also, research topics of interest.

These sites are powerful search engines in their own right, so posting content relevant to your business—mortgage and primarily real estate—with relevant keywords and hashtags that coincide with the search terms you'd like to come up for—can help you drive more traffic and get you more leads when people are searching on these websites for information relevant to mortgage and real estate services in your local area.

Reviews

People can't review your website through sites like Yelp, but they can rate your business.

Review websites, especially Yelp, place extremely well for many branded and unbranded mortgage and real estate related keywords.

If your business has a lot of good reviews and your website URL is included in your profile, you can gain more credibility, traffic, and leads through this social influencer.

Blogs

These days there are blogs covering pretty much any topic you could possibly imagine. You don't have to create a blog to take advantage of the SEO benefits they can provide.

What you want to do is get your page linked on relevant, good quality blogs, especially ones related to your keyword goals.

Most blog posts allow comments, which can be a great place to show your expertise and also include links back to your website or landing page.

The key, as always, is to look for the highest quality blogs and share good information and valuable content that can be helpful to the blog's audience.

Spamming

It can be very easy to try and take short cuts here.

You could literally blast tons of blogs with links to your website, or you could create a whole bunch of social media accounts, then share a link to your website on them, and even create fake reviews...

However, this will only hurt your search engine goals.

Search engines are very aware of these shortcuts and are always looking out for them. They will catch you.

Don't try to outsmart Google or you will get penalized and possibly blacklisted.

Local SEO

While there are many similarities between traditional and local SEO, there are also many differences.

When potential borrowers are searching locally, chances are they're close making a purchase and looking for a company or individual in their local area to work with.

That's why it's crucial that the search engines have a clear understanding of what your business does and where you are located.

The "Google 3-Pack," (Figure 20-3) is what comes up for searches like, "San Diego mortgage company"—directly beneath the paid ads and above the natural search engine results pages.

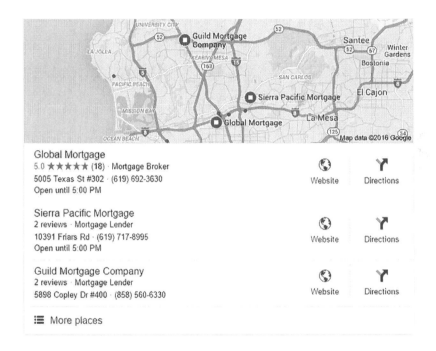

Figure 20-3: example of "Google 3-Pack" local listing display shown on results pages.

Local search engine placement is based off of the physical location of your business.

If your business is located in San Diego and you want to be found for local searches in Boston, that's not going to happen.

Before you start any work on local SEO, you have to make sure you've registered your business with the major search engines.

Without doing this, your business will not show up in local SEO results.

To register, you will have to fill out some information on your company, and in most cases, the search engines will send you a postcard with a unique PIN number that you'll need to enter to verify your business.

For Google and Bing, follow the steps outlined on the sites below:

► www.google.com/business
► www.bingplaces.com

When you're setting up your business profile with search engines, it's important to fill out all the fields that they offer.

A full profile will always look better to the search engines compared to one that's incomplete.

When creating your strategy for local SEO, here are some important points you'll want to follow:

Name, Address, and Phone Number (NAP)

Your company's name, address, and phone number, or "NAP" as it is commonly referred to, need to be accurate and consistent across all online references.

Not only on your local SEO profiles with search engines, but also on your website and any other reference to your business online.

In these geo-targeted searches, search engines cross-reference your NAP on many different online sites, and consistency will help validate your business.

On-Page Website Optimization

Your website's on-page optimization is also an important influencer on search engines when it comes to Local SEO.

When search engines index your website, they will look for NAP consistency and also keywords in your tags. Also, they'll index the content of your website to match the keywords and geographic area you are looking to be found for.

Off-Page Website Signals

As mentioned, it's important to have accurate NAP listings on various online websites to improve your chances at better local SEO placement.

Besides that, and similar to traditional SEO, quality links pointing back to your website are also strong validation points for search engines when it comes to local SEO

Top 15 Local Search Ranking Factors (according to Moz.com)

1. Physical address in city of search
2. Consistency of structured citations
3. Proper "Google my Business" (GMB) category associations
4. Proximity of address to the point of search
5. Quality/authority of structured citations
6. Domain authority of website
7. Product/service keyword in GMB title
8. City, state in GMB landing page title
9. HTML name, address, phone (NAP), matching GMB location NAP
10. Click-through rate (CTR) from search results
11. Quantity of native Google reviews (w/ text)
12. Quality/authority of inbound links to domain
13. Individually owner-verified GMB location

14. Quantity of structured citations (Internet Yellow Pages, Data Aggregators)

15. Quality/authority of inbound links to GMB landing page URL

Common SEO Mistakes

There's a lot of bad information out there when it comes to search engine optimization. Not to mention, in many cases, tactics that worked last year (or even a few months ago) won't necessarily work anymore this year.

Mistakes are easy to fall into and they can hurt your chances of showing up in search engines, which will make SEO frustrating and seem like a waste of time.

Telling Google you "didn't know" won't help you if you get penalized, so make sure you avoid these common mistakes:

Having Unrealistic Expectations

I talked about this a little bit in the introduction to this chapter, but it's worth repeating as it's one of the most common mistakes mortgage professionals and business owners, in general, who are new to SEO make.

It's important not to go after keywords and phrases that are incredibly competitive, which you'll have little to no chance at coming up for organically if you don't have the budget for it.

For example: if you're licensed to do loans in California, it makes sense to want to be found anytime anyone in California searches for a mortgage.

Unfortunately, it's not that easy.

Think about how many people sell mortgages in California, including national lenders and banks, and also mortgage lead generation companies all targeting California mortgage related searches...

The more competitive a search term is, the harder it will be to get top 10 placement for organically.

There Are No SEO Shortcuts

Like most things in life, with SEO, there are no shortcuts. You might find different articles or certain SEO companies claiming they've figured out some magic formula... Don't believe them.

Search engines are aggressively fighting anything they view as an attempt to game the system.

Cheating won't just not help you, it will actually hurt you, and can result in your website being removed from search engines altogether.

Common SEO shortcuts to avoid are:

- ▶ Paying for backlinks
- ▶ Stealing content from other websites and putting it on yours
- ▶ Not taking the time to write high quality, unique content
- ▶ Including too many keyword phrases in your content, also known as "keyword stuffing"
- ▶ Spamming social media sites and blogs with links back to your website

It can be extremely disheartening when you work for a goal and don't see any progress, so be realistic and strategic with your SEO plans by going after less competitive, local terms; be patient, work hard, and if it sounds too good to be true, it most definitely is.

CHAPTER 21

Citation & Review Collection/ORM Strategy (Online Reputation Management)

Your reputation is everything. What's crazy is that these days, your online reputation can be even more important than your offline reputation.

The reason is whereas an unhappy client could traditionally only reach maybe a handful of people previously, in today's social media and online review world, they can reach hundreds, even thousands at a time... and their comments and opinions can last indefinitely.

I shared some statistics about consumer behavior a couple times in this *Manifesto*, including the percentage of people who go online to research a company before doing business—a whopping 97% of those surveyed, and also, the number of people that trust online reviews as much as personal recommendations—88% of those surveyed...

In business, it has always been imperative to offer great service—be honest, prompt, courteous, follow-up, and to always go the extra mile for clients and business partners.

Your online reputation can magnify these qualities and behaviors, for better or for worse.

That's why, now more than ever, it's absolutely crucial that if you mess something up, you own up to it, and do everything in your power to make it right.

A good strategy to implement is to have a feedback/survey mechanism for clients during and after the sales process so that you can be proactive and put out fires before they become explosions.

You can also address issues with clients directly—often building a stronger relationship with them—before they decide to go online and write something that can have a negative (and lasting) effect on your business.

Chapter 34 of this *Manifesto* includes a bunch of great tools I recommend, many of which my team and I use daily. There you'll find some online reputation management (ORM) tools that can help you collect reviews, monitor online chatter, and get real-time feedback from clients and partners you're working with.

In terms of ORM, think of the first page of Google as incredibly valuable real estate.

When someone Googles your name and/or business, it's critical that you "own" as many of the top listings as possible, and that those top listings are positive, current, and accurate in terms of the information one might find upon clicking into them.

Below are some free and powerful websites you can create profiles on to help you better control what comes up when people search for you online.

Some of them are obvious; others, not so much. The key is they're all trusted websites and domains with strong authority that rank well in Google.

As you setup profiles on various websites, remember to keep a consistent NAP (name, email, phone number) or you'll hurt your SEO efforts.

25 Powerful Citation Websites

1. ActiveRain
2. AngiesList
3. BBB
4. BingPlaces
5. CitySearch
6. Clarity.fm
7. Facebook
8. FindTheBest (Graphiq)
9. Google+
10. Indeed
11. Kudzu
12. JudysBook
13. LinkedIn
14. Local
15. Manta
16. Pinterest
17. SlideShare
18. Spokeo
19. SuperPages
20. TrustPilot
21. Twitter
22. YahooLocal
23. Yelp
24. YouTube
25. YP

For a list of these websites online, go to:

www.leadPops.com/reputation-management

CHAPTER 22
Google Pay Per Click Mortgage Advertising

G oogle pay per click (PPC) can be a super profitable loan-getting channel, but you need to know what you're doing and what you're up against, or else you will burn through a boatload of cash with nothing to show for it—quickly.

There's figuring out which keywords not only drive traffic, but actually convert into leads.

You also need to know where to target geographically to get the most bang for your buck, and what times of day and days of the week convert best so you can focus your budget on what's actually bringing in business.

On top of that, you've got to dial in your landing page quality scores, otherwise Google will penalize you and place you beneath competitors who are actually paying less per click than you.

And that goes hand-in-hand with the top priority before launching PPC or any other type of marketing—optimizing to make sure you're going to convert leads before your turn on the campaign.

You can't sell a mortgage to a click, and getting a bunch of traffic and exposure without converting leads is like pouring water into a bucket that's full of holes.

Bonus: My Mortgage PPC Cheatsheet will help you hit the ground running when it comes to PPC advertising on Google:

www.leadPops.com/manifesto-bonus

*Recommended minimum Google PPC ad spend:

$3k+ per month for at least 90 days to give yourself an opportunity to gather data and get results.

CHAPTER 23

Use Signage with Your Domain

S ignage, posters, and stickers can be used at your office, events, on your vehicle, license plate holders, banners at youth sports games, and much more.

It's crucial that any marketing you use includes your domain name, ly with a strong call-to-action to give people a reason to check you out online.

A good domain name is much easier to remember than a phone number, and a lot less intimidating for a potential client to visit on their own terms vs. having to talk to a salesperson.

If the destination you drive them to (whether it's a website, microsite, or landing page) is optimized to convert leads, you'll have a great opportunity to generate more business as a result of using signage as a part of your marketing.

Here are some websites to help get you going (no affiliation to leadPops):

▶ www.StickerMule.com
▶ www.VistaPrint.com

Shopping Cart Advertising

Shopping cart ads can give you exposure to a captive audience in your local market and beyond.

Here's a website to help get you going:

www.Cartvertising.com (no affiliation to leadPops)

Billboard, Car Wash, Bench, & Gas Pump Advertising

Billboards, car washes, benches, and gas pump ads can also give you great exposure to a captive audience.

Here are some websites to help get you going (no affiliation to leadPops):

- ► www.BlueLineMedia.com
- ► www.ClearChannelOutdoor.com
- ► www.CreativeDisplayAds.com
- ► www.Lamar.com
- ► www.OutFrontMedia.com

CHAPTER 24

Sponsor a Local School, Church, Little League, Golf Tournament, Martial Arts Studio, etc.

S ponsoring a local organization is a great way to give back to a community, while at the same time getting more exposure for your business.

It creates good will and can provide a lot of opportunities to promote your brand with signage, plaques, jerseys, trophies, flyers, benches, posters, photographs, calendars, banners, bulletins, events, and more.

Come up with a list of some causes you can get behind in your local area and look for sponsorship opportunities on their website or by meeting with organization managers/directors.

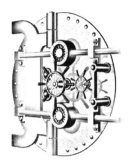

CHAPTER 25
Movie Theater Events & Advertising

Here are a couple ideas for movie theater marketing:

► Advertise on screen before films

► Rent out a theater and invite past clients and business partners for a private showing

Here are some websites to help you get going (no affiliation to leadPops):

► www.Cinemark.com

► www.NCM.com

Look for information on "Private Events" and/or "Advertising".

CHAPTER 26

Local Publication & Magazine Advertising

I n most areas, local publications like newspapers and magazines are still a viable advertising opportunity.

Not only are many paper publications still in circulation (with readers—be sure to get numbers on that before you invest), but they usually also have a digital version, which can be another untapped place to advertise that your competitors have not taken advantage of.

As always, use a strong call-to-action, integrate a conversion-optimized website, microsite, or landing page to direct consumers to, and be sure to research the publication's demographics so that you come up with ads that are relevant to the audience.

Also, remember to check out the "Ideal Customer Persona" bonus, perfect for helping you determine exactly who you're targeting and what type of offer you should put together for each campaign:

www.leadPops.com/manifesto-bonus

One more thing: I've created a page with some resources to help you get going with local publication advertising, including lists of all regional and local magazines and newspapers in the US:

www.leadPops.com/magazine-ads

CHAPTER 27
Charity, Donations, & Goodwill

It goes without saying, donating to charitable organizations and causes is a good thing to do.

When used tactfully, it also help incentivize potential clients to work with you, feeling that they're giving through your donation in a world where so many companies and individuals only care about profit.

You can offer to donate whatever amount you choose to a charity that you pick, or let your clients choose which charity they want you to make the donation to.

This can be a promotion you run once or twice a year, for a month or a week at a time—however often and long you want—it's entirely up to you, of course.

You can offer to make a donation for every quote, closed loan, referral, etc.—in whatever amount you choose.

Here's a website to help you pick reputable charities:

www.CharityNavigator.org (no affiliation to leadPops)

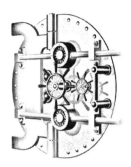

CHAPTER 28

Traditional & Internet Radio Advertising

M any mortgage professionals I've worked with over the years have absolutely crushed it with radio ads.

With a strong radio presence and consistent messaging, you can practically cement your business into the minds of listeners that are loyal to the station(s) you advertise on.

When advertising on the radio, it's crucial to emphasize a good web address with a strong call-to-action, and not just promote a phone number.

Of course you'd prefer phone calls, but it's not about what you want. It's about what potential borrowers are most likely to respond to.

A good web address is a lot easier to remember than a phone number, and as mentioned in some of the earlier chapters, consumers these days want to go online and do their research before calling up a sales organization—especially for something like a mortgage.

To get the best possible results, use a good domain name and drive consumers to a dedicated landing page that reflects the offer and messaging of the radio ad.

You can also drive people directly to your website homepage. If you do, just make sure that your homepage is optimized to convert leads, and that you've got a clear reference to the radio station on there.

Use "As heard on..." with the radio station's logo, and consistent messaging (ad-scent)—which applies to all forms of marketing, including radio.

In conjunction with radio ads, I recommend simultaneously running a PPC campaign for branded key phrases (your name and/ or company name) so that potential clients who don't type in your domain name, but instead, Google you (because they keep hearing your business on the radio), can be driven to your landing page or website as well.

When someone is searching for you on Google, the more of the first page you take up, the better. Having an ad spot at the top, as well as the first organic listing, will help you bring in more business.

Not to mention branded keywords are very cheap compared to unbranded mortgage keywords and phrases.

With radio ads, it's important to be selective with your demographics.

Just because a radio station has a large listenership doesn't mean that it is going to get you in front of your ideal target audience.

For example: AM political talk radio will usually get you in front of a smaller audience, but at the same time, a much higher likelihood that a larger percentage of the people listening to AM political talk radio are qualified for a mortgage or refinance than people listening to a pop station (in most cases).

Remember to get your "Ideal Customer Persona" bonus workbook:

www.leadPops.com/manifesto-bonus

Here are some websites to help you get going with radio advertising (no affiliation to leadPops):

- ► www.AmericasTalkRadioNetwork.com/advertising
- ► www.BizTalkRadio.com/contact
- ► www.CBSRadio.com/advertise
- ► www.Cumulus.com/local-radio
- ► www.iHeartMedia.com
- ► www.Jelli.com
- ► www.MarketingArchitects.com
- ► advertising.Pandora.com (no "www.")
- ► www.PremiereNetworks.com
- ► www.PushButtonProductions.com
- ► www.RedStateTalkRadio.com
- ► www.SiriusXM.com/advertise
- ► www.Slacker.com/advertise
- ► www.StrategicMediaInc.com
- ► www.TRN1.com
- ► www.VoiceAmerica.com
- ► www.WestStar.com
- ► www.WestwoodOne.com

For a list of these websites online, go to:

www.leadPops.com/mortgage-radio-ads

CHAPTER 29

Canvassing Communities, Stadiums, Events, Festivals, Parking Lots, Convention Centers, etc.

You can get your offer in front of hundreds if not thousands of potential clients by utilizing a canvassing service to hand out your materials (flyers, mailers, door hangers, etc.) or put them on front doors and vehicles in parking lots—anywhere there's a large gathering of people.

Like with all other ads, canvassing materials should always emphasize a good web address with a strong call-to-action, and not just promote a phone number.

Simply Google the phrase "canvassing services" if you're interested in canvassing:

You can also find somebody to help you locally off of a website like Craigslist, or even hire some (dependable) high school or college kids to do the work for you.

CHAPTER 30

Branded Apparel, Stationery, Calendars, Pens & Pads, Magnets, & Other Swag

W hen done right, branded swag can be a cool marketing tool and also have a lasting effect in promoting your business.

As always, make sure you include your domain name on any promotional material.

Here are some websites to help you get going (no affiliation to leadPops):

- ► www.Deluxe.com
- ► www.Nadel.com
- ► www.PinnaclePromotions.com
- ► www.VistaPrint.com

CHAPTER 31

Automatically Send Personalized Cards & Gifts

P ersonalized outreach can go a long way when it comes to helping you build stronger, longer-lasting relationships with clients and referral partners.

Add automation to the mix, and you've got a powerful strategy that can truly separate you from your competitors.

Check out a website called:

www.SendOutCards.com (no affiliation to leadPops)

In less than 60 seconds, you can choose your custom card, add a personal photo, write your heartfelt, inspirational, or cheerful message, and click send.

They print, stuff, stamp, and mail your personalized greeting cards to any postal address anywhere in the world, all for less than the average price of a greeting card at the store.

They also offer a gift selection, which is like icing on the cake to this cool service.

CHAPTER 32
Content Distribution Network Advertising

C ontent marketing is another great way to promote your business—allowing you to tell a good story, educate potential clients, and create value for your audience.

Content distribution networks (CDNs) offer personalized content recommendations, placing ads within the context of a users' experience—often embedded on websites surrounded by other content (non-ads), blending in and making the ad feel less disruptive and more like part of a discovery process.

This increases the chances that potential clients will click-through into your content.

CDNs show their ads at the bottom of trusted websites like CNN, ESPN, Huffington Post, etc., using various algorithms to help match the ad displayed to the interests of users consuming the non-paid content, helping advertisers monetize their content and drive higher engagement.

Figure 32-1: real content on Time.com shows on the left, while content from the CDN, "Outbrain", shows along the right. Notice how similar the formatting on the right is to that on the left.

Here are the top content distribution networks (no affiliation to leadPops):

- ► www.AdBlade.com
- ► www.Gravity.com
- ► www.Outbrain.com
- ► www.Taboola.com
- ► www.Zemanta.com

CHAPTER 33

Corporate & Association Affinity Marketing

Affinity marketing can be a powerful way to get you in front of a lot of people at once, instead of just one prospect at a time.

With affinity marketing, you partner with employers and associations to offer their employees and members benefits that you choose.

For example: an offer to waive the loan origination fee, or some other discounted membership perk like a credit towards closing costs, a free mortgage consultation, a home ownership webinar or seminar, a free credit analysis, etc.

To add more value to your offering, team up with other local service providers and professionals, each offering a discount or some sort of deal to the employees or members.

Key partners to add to your affinity marketing team include each of the following: Realtor®, insurance agent, moving company, contractor, financial advisor, cleaning service, personal trainer, home inspector, real estate attorney, divorce attorney, landscaper, pest control company, dentist, solar company, HVAC, plumber, painter, and/or anyone else you can think of that can add value.

With affinity marketing, everyone wins—the employers/ associations, the employees/members, you, and your affinity marketing team.

You can often negotiate with employers to present your program in a variety of ways, including but not limited to: brochures/flyers, webinars/seminars, lunch and learns, posters, payroll stuffers, featured placement in corporate intranets, email marketing campaigns, company events, and much more.

To start, simply line up 5-10+ local partners you can team up with and make a list of local employers and associations that you can target, ideally each with dozens or even hundreds or thousands of employees or members.

Create a quick PowerPoint presentation or use www.SlideShare.net (no affiliation to leadPops) to outline your offering.

Be sure to get contact information, including email addresses, for each employer/association director and all their employees/ members, segmented in your database so you can quickly and easily communicate updates, such as special offers, new service providers, upcoming events, and more.

To make your affinity marketing program even better, create a simple microsite specific to each employer/association director.

This gives them a destination to drive their employees/members to that offers information on all the benefits provided by your program, and a signup form for new employees to enroll 24/7.

CHAPTER 34
Awesome, Life-Changing Marketing Automation & Efficiency Tools

This entire list is comprised of tools that have changed my life as a business owner and marketer... And that's not an overstatement.

I've used everything on this list personally and continue to use most of these tools on a regular basis.

I believe in them enough to share them with you here, and also run affiliate links for many of them, which is about as high of a recommendation as I can offer for a 3rd party solution.

Check them out. It will definitely be worth your time.

For an easy, clickable list of these websites online, go to:

www.leadPops.com/awesome-tools

CONTENT CREATION

iWriter: articles, blog posts, press releases, and more
www.iWriter.com (only hire "Elite" writers)

Scripted: where marketers and writers work together
www.Scripted.com

Textbroker: authors deliver high-quality content
www.Textbroker.com

DESIGN TOOLS & SERVICES

99 Designs: logo and graphic design services
www.99Designs.com

Canva: create banner ads and other designs
www.Canva.com

EMAIL MARKETING & LIST BUILDING

Email Fire™: email marketing and automation
www.leadPops.com/email-fire

HelloBar: list building tools
www.HelloBar.com

OptiMonk: exit intent pop-ups and other list building tools
www.OptiMonk.com

Sleeknote: more list building tools
www.Sleeknote.com

YesWare: track email opens, reply rates, link clicks, attachment opens, and more
www.YesWare.com

LANDING PAGES & LEAD CAPTURE FORMS

Mortgage Funnels: 32 mortgage and real estate lead generation landing pages ready to deploy in 5 minutes or less
www.MortgageFunnels.com

PagePops: 150+ fully customizable landing page and microsite templates featuring a simple drag and drop editor
www.leadPops.com/PagePops

LIVE CHAT

ZopIM: greet your customers instantly with live chat
www.ZopIM.com

MEETINGS & APPOINTMENTS

JoinMe: screen sharing and conference software
www.Join.me

YouCanBookMe: customer bookings straight into your calendar
www.YouCanBook.me

ONLINE REPUTATION MANAGEMENT & REVIEWS

SocialSurvey: Manage online reputation and capture data
to create a winning social strategy and boost customer satisfaction
across the Enterprise
www.SocialSurvey.com

RETARGETING PLATFORMS

Adroll: top retargeting platform
www.AdRoll.com

Perfect Audience: mobile, web, and Facebook retargeting
www.PerfectAudience.com

SiteScout: self-serve advertising and retargeting
www.SiteScout.com

SEARCH ENGINE MARKETING & KEYWORD RESEARCH

iSpionage: steal your competitors' traffic and uncover their conversion strategy
www.iSpionage.com

SEMRush: SEO keyword research and competitor search engine data
www.SEMRush.com

SpyFu: SEO competitor analysis and research tools
www.SpyFu.com

SOCIAL MEDIA TOOLS

Buffer: awesome social media sharing
www.Buffer.com

Clyxo: display your social profiles on one simple page
www.Clyxo.com

Sniply: add a branded call-to-action to every link you share
www.Snip.ly

StatusBrew: grow your followers on Twitter and Instagram
www.StatusBrew.com

STOCK PHOTOGRAPHY

PicMonkey: online image editing, collages, and more
www.PicMonkey.com

Pixabay: free images and videos you can use anywhere
www.Pixabay.com

ShutterStock: beautiful images you pay for
www.ShutterStock.com

TinyJPG: smart PNG and JPEG image compression
www.TinyJPG.com

Unsplash: free high-resolution photos
www.Unsplash.com

TRACKING, TESTING, & HEATMAPS

Google Analytics: track website visitors, conversations, and much
more
www.Google.com/analytics

Google Tag Manager: launch new tags and tracking pixels quickly
www.google.com/analytics/tag-manager/

Hotjar: heatmaps, click tracking, visitor screen recording, and much more
www.HotJar.com

Optimizely: A/B testing software
www.Optimizely.com

VIDEO MARKETING

Veeroll: generate video ads automatically
www.VeeRoll.com

Wistia: video marketing for business
www.Wistia.com

VIRTUAL ASSISTANTS& OUTSOURCING

Fiverr: marketplace for creative and professional services starting at $5
www.Fiverr.com

Upwork: hire expert virtual assistants around the world
www.Upwork.com

Virtual Staff Finder: professional virtual assistant headhunters
www.VirtualStaffFinder.com

OTHER COOL TOOLS

ActiveProspect: proof of consent and TCPA compliance for lead
forms
www.ActiveProspect.com

Agent Legend: automatically send personalized voice mails, text
messages, and emails without lifting a finger
www.AgentLegend.com

Audible: download audiobooks to any listening device
www.Audible.com

Bond: send handwritten notes on customizable stationery
www.Bond.co

Evernote: collect, nurture, and share ideas across desktop and
mobile platforms
www.Evernote.com

Honey: automatically find and apply coupon codes when you shop
online
www.JoinHoney.com

IFTTT: connect apps and devices you love with
"if this, then that" statements
www.IFTTT.com

Ninja Outreach: find influencers and automate outreach
www.NinjaOutreach.com

Spreengs: share a digital video in a card
www.Spreengs.com

TechSmith (Jing): screenshot and screencast software
www.TechSmith.com/Jing

Taskworld: empowers your team to finish work on time, measure
performance and accomplish great results
www.Taskworld.com

Udemy: business relevant, professional-grade courses
and training content
www.Udemy.com

WebinarJam: webinar technology
www.WebinarJam.com

Xverify: real-time lead data validation
www.Xverify.com

CHAPTER 35
Mortgage Funnels

At this point, I've covered dozens of different strategies and ideas to help you grow your mortgage business.

Though they range from traditional advertising to digital marketing and referral generation, they all share one major thing in common:

You need optimized lead generation tools, otherwise you're wasting time and money, and you're losing clients.

If you're like most mortgage professionals I've worked with over the last decade, you have neither the time nor the inclination to figure out how to create high-converting landing pages and lead generation forms.

You're busy enough as is communicating with clients and referral partners, and closing loans...

The problem is: without these important tools, you're spinning your wheels when it comes to your marketing, and missing out on opportunities to do more business daily.

Loans you should be closing are getting snatched up by the likes of LendingTree and Zillow.

<u>Not</u> cool.

That's why I created Mortgage Funnels—the <u>only</u> plug-and-play lead generation and marketing system in the mortgage industry that's specifically built to make it easy and fun for your customers to request personalized help from you.

This is the same technology some of the biggest players in the industry are using to generate their leads...

I know because I've developed lead generation tools for a whole bunch of them!

Mortgage Funnels are 100% custom designed for YOUR specific needs as a mortgage originator, so they blow away the standard "one-size-fits-all" lead forms that generic landing page software spits out...

AND the wannabe lead capture forms "built into" those mortgage website templates.

On that note, if you've been disappointed with the leads from your mortgage website, these funnels are exactly what you've been missing all along.

Mortgage Funnels are fast and easy to deploy in your business—they plug right into your existing marketing in less than 5 minutes.

And because I've refined and tuned these funnels through hundreds of tests, they work like crazy for pretty much every LO that tries them.

It's like releasing the emergency brake that has been slowing your marketing to a crawl—suddenly every dollar you spend on ads generates as much as 2-4X more leads.

That's what conversion optimization is all about—compelling potential clients to take action, and getting the most out of everything you do to promote and grow your business.

Mortgage Funnels connect you with your potential client so that you can do what you do best—build a relationship, help them with their mortgage, and make some decent money while you're at it.

Here's how it all works:

When a home owner or home buyer visits your Mortgage Funnels, she sees a friendly invitation to answer a few non-intrusive questions... Presented in a way that's enticing...

And with each question she answers, the Mortgage Funnel "rewards" her progress.

She's tweaking menus and adjusting sliders, almost like she's customizing the options on a new family sedan...

She's having FUN—while she's giving you all the information you need to qualify her for a home loan.

She gets more and more engrossed, and before she knows it, she's at the point of no return...

And since you've built a relationship with her by focusing on HER needs, at the end, she's happy to fill in her name, phone number, and email address.

Now on the surface this looks like a simple process, but there's some deep psychology at work here.

Every part of your Mortgage Funnels is carefully designed and tested...

The wording of the questions. The colors of the buttons and where elements are positioned on the page. Weird things you'd probably never think of, like hover effects, instant answer validation, hot keys... Subtle animations and interactions to help guide potential clients along...

Even the order of the questions themselves can make or break your success.

It ALL matters. And it's all precision-tuned to pull your visitors in and gets them click-click-clicking along...

Build a relationship by getting a dozen or so "easy yeses" first to get their buy-in <u>before</u> asking for sensitive information...

And once they're invested in the process, they'll be more than happy to share their email and phone number so you can follow-up with them.

That means more leads—in many cases 2-4 times more—from the SAME advertising budget.

But the sheer number of leads you'll get isn't even the most exciting part...

For one thing, these leads are 100% YOURS.

YOU generated these leads through your marketing, and you'll never have to scratch and claw with 15 other LOs to close them.

Then there's the lead quality.

First off, you get MUCH more than just a name and phone number.

You'll have at your fingertips all the information you need to instantly sort the closable customers from the hopeless lost causes.

And when you pick up the phone, these people are EXPECTING to hear from you, and they're HAPPY to talk to you.

That's right—no more playing phone tag with tire-kickers who dodge you and "screen" your calls.

Instead they'll be impressed and appreciative of your outstanding customer service.

Everybody wins:

Your customers are happy because they actually enjoyed the experience of requesting a quote—without going through a mortgage telesales slaughterhouse to get the info they wanted.

And you're happy because you're getting truly EXCLUSIVE leads, including all the data you need to provide an accurate quote—and then connecting with real human beings instead of getting the voicemail cold-shoulder.

There's so much more that goes into (and comes with) Mortgage Funnels...

I don't want to get into all the details here in this chapter.

Rather, I'd like to just provide you with a quick introduction to the Mortgage Funnels platform and let you know that it was created just for you.

If you don't have a Mortgage Funnels account yet, learn more, and signup for free at:

www.MortgageFunnels.com

Conclusion

ongratulations, you've made it to the end... or actually, I should say: the <u>beginning</u>!

My goal with this book is to have given you a marketing roadmap with an emphasis on building your foundation, and understanding that without it, none of your marketing and business development efforts will perform like you expect them to... like you <u>need</u> them to.

I hope that I've given you that, and much more.

I also hope your head isn't about to explode, because now it's time to take all the stuff you've learned, and begin applying it to your daily business.

It might seem like a lot to take in, but remember:

Start with the right foundation—one designed to capture and convert leads by making it easy for potential clients to say "yes" to giving you their information—and everything else will fall into place.

The days of just crossing your fingers and hoping that people will call because you send them an email every few weeks, or because a couple real estate agents hand out your business cards here and there, are over.

It's time to be strategic with everything that you do to promote and grow your business.

Look at what you're currently spending time and money on in terms of marketing and business development, and ask yourself these questions:

- ▶ When people see my ad, open my email, come to my website or blog—whatever it might be—am I engaging them quickly and efficiently?

- ▶ Am I using the same strategies to convert qualified leads that have been proven by the most successful marketers in the mortgage industry?

If the answer is "no", get excited...

That means with just a few slight tweaks to stuff you're already doing, you could double or triple... even quadruple your business.

But you have to start approaching your marketing with a mindset of ROI and optimization, not just "hope and pray" tactics.

Here are your next steps:

1. First, you need to setup lead conversion tools.

2. Next, you need to start plugging those lead conversion tools into the marketing that you're already doing...

   Stuff like emails, website content, blogs, social media posts, videos, PPC, retargeting, Realtor® conversations, your email signature, voicemail messages, etc.

3. You can't help people by just giving them good content. This is why it's imperative you make it ridiculously easy for them to get in touch with you (and not just by picking up the phone and calling you, or filling out your 1003).

4. Optimize everything with good calls-to-action, plus buttons and links that take potential clients to

landing pages with interactive forms to collect their information.

Once you have their information, get these people on the phone quickly and do what you do best: build relationships, and help them with their financial goals.

Don't leave anything to chance.

Learn from the big companies that have spent the last 10-20 years figuring out how to make money online in the mortgage industry, and use their marketing and lead generation tactics to your advantage.

That doesn't mean you should go posting 2% mortgage rates to get your phone to ring, either.

It does mean: optimize your efforts so that you can work with more people that need your help, and stop losing out on business to companies just because they have better marketing and lead generation strategies than you.

Liftoff

Some of you that are self-starters and good with marketing and technology will begin incorporating these strategies immediately.

For you, results will come quickly... Oftentimes same day. I see it all the time.

I'd love to hear how you're doing and what's working best. You can email me anytime—Andrew@leadPops.com.

Others will read this book, shrug their shoulders, and go back to "business as usual".

That's OK, too. Optimizing to get the best results isn't for everyone.

Then there are some of you that are reading this, who understand the power of the strategies I've shared in this book and want to take the necessary steps to begin increasing your marketing ROI and business, but would like one-on-one coaching and hands on assistance to incorporate these tactics into your business...

If that's you, I've created something incredibly valuable for you.

It's called Mortgage Marketing Liftoff.

Liftoff is a private mastermind group made up of:

- ► 1:1 Coaching
- ► Technology
- ► Implementation

My team and I will get on the phone with you personally for 1 hour and create what's called a SWOT Analysis, allowing us to uncover strengths, weaknesses, opportunities, and threats in your business.

We'll share those results with you in a detailed report, along with a plan to help you capitalize on your strengths and opportunities, while minimizing (and in many cases, eliminating) weaknesses and threats.

Then, my team and I will come alongside you to break through any sticking points you have with your marketing, and work with you for 12 months to help you build your foundation and optimize everything that you're doing—from email marketing to social media, Realtor® relationships to offline marketing, and everything in between.

If this sounds like something you're interested in, I invite you to apply with me personally here:

www.leadPops.com/Liftoff

Once you apply, my team will follow-up with you to discuss the program and see if it's a fit.

If it is, we'll schedule your first call to learn about you and your goals, and then we'll conduct your SWOT Analysis shortly thereafter.

So now, the next steps are up to you.

I urge you to take what you've learned and begin incorporating these strategies into your business TODAY.

Don't wait, act NOW, while this information is still fresh.

Keep this book nearby and reference it often, at least until "conversion optimization" becomes second nature for you.

Remember: a few small changes can make a HUGE difference in the amount of loans you're closing each month.

Once you understand that, you'll start uncovering the many opportunities to get better results that are all around you.

I wish you all the success in the world.

—Andrew Pawlak

Acknowledgements

A lot of people have inspired me over the years. Some of them know it, some of them don't. I'd like to take this opportunity to share their names in this section.

First, my right-hand guys: Peter Barankiewicz and Charles Dean. You rock. It's hard to imagine such a small group can grind so hard and get so much done, while having such a great time "working" together. I couldn't ask for more.

There are several other people that have had a positive impact on my life, and that I'd like to thank for their help and support (in no particular order):

Tamara Pawlak, Danuta Pawlak, Rosa Romaine, Fritz Hottenstein, Bob and Lou Anne Davis, John and Lynn Traylor, Robert Pilc, Muhammad Nouman, Sal Nouman, Steele Rocky, Brian Tracy, Frank Kern, Joshua Earl, Matt Howard, Pat Howard, Myles Vives, Ryan Stewman, Nick Davis, Brandon Stigers, Steve Weber, Stephen Capezza, Ed O'Neil, Bob Hart, Rhonda Anderson, Colin Treend, Paul Allen, Bill Burnett, Joe Giamanco, Kellie Shuey, Paul Duncan, Brad Costanzo, Jill McKellan, and Oliver James.

And finally, I'd also like to thank all of my clients. You are the reason why my team and I work so hard, and absolutely love what we do.

I'm excited to keep wowing you with new and improved products and services for years to come.

About Andrew Pawlak

ANDREW PAWLAK is a passionate idea guy, and more importantly, he's an executor.

As an entrepreneur with 12 years of sales and digital marketing experience, Andrew has been a pioneer in conversion optimization for mortgage and real estate marketing since starting in the industry in 2004.

He has co-founded 2 successful internet startups in the mortgage space, including leadPops, Inc., where he's the CEO.

Andrew has consulted thousands of independent loan officers, real estate agents, and insurance agents, as well as c-level executives at publicly traded companies in the mortgage and real estate industries.

Technology Andrew has developed has generated over $250,000,000 in sales commissions for clients nationwide.

Today, he and his team offer training, consulting, and lead generation technology to loan officers, Realtors, and insurance agents all over the country, with over $2M in leads running through their systems each month.

In 2013, Andrew married his soulmate of 11 years, Ashley.

A favorite quote he lives by is from Zig Ziglar:

"You will get all you want in life if you help enough other people get what they want."

Andrew is always open to discussions about marketing and business development.

You can connect with Andrew by going to:

- ▶ Website—www.leadPops.com
- ▶ Twitter—www.Twitter.com/AndrewPawlakLP
- ▶ LinkedIn—www.LinkedIn.com/in/AndrewPawlak
- ▶ Blog—www.HailToTheHustle.com

Manifesto Resource Links

For an online directory of these links, go to:

www.leadPops.com/manifesto-resources

Resource Links by Chapter:

Chapter 1:

www.MortgagePops.com

www.leadPops.com/big-dogs

www.leadPops.com/mobile-website-test

www.leadPops.com/credit-repair

www.SuperCalc.io

www.leadPops.com/manifesto-bonus

www.leadPops.com/website-grader

Chapter 3:

www.leadPops.com/mortgage-crm-list

Chapter 6:

www.leadPops.com/pro-email

Chapter 8:

www.leadPops.com/manifesto-updates

www.leadPops.com/clear-cookies

Chapter 12:

www.leadPops.com/find-realtor-websites

Chapter 15:

www.leadPops.com/mortgage-rate-tables

Chapter 16:

www.leadPops.com/pagepops

Chapter 21:

www.leadPops.com/reputation-management

Chapter 26:

www.leadPops.com/magazine-ads

Chapter 28:

www.leadPops.com/mortgage-radio-ads

Chapter 34:

www.leadPops.com/awesome-tools

Chapter 35:

www.MortgageFunnels.com

Conclusion:

www.leadPops.com/liftoff

Made in the USA
Columbia, SC
16 December 2020